Seeking the Amazing

Seeking the Amazing

RACHEL BRAMBLE

JANUS PUBLISHING COMPANY
London, England

First Published in Great Britain 2005
by Janus Publishing Company Ltd,
105-107 Gloucester Place,
London W1U 6BY

www.januspublishing.co.uk

British Library Cataloguing-in-Publication Data
A catalogue record for this book
is available from the British Library

ISBN 1 85756 625 4

Cover Design Simon Hughes

Printed and bound in Great Britain

Forward

In October 2002 I found out the truth that my partner had been cheating on me throughout our relationship.

I had met him through a chat room on the Internet.

I had two children aged 10 and 12 years old and anticipated a life on my own once more; I went on dating sites in the vague hope that this time I might be more lucky. It was a way of passing the time and a distraction from my loneliness, disappointment and coming to terms with the truth.

This is a true account of my journey through internet dating over a period of about six months and records both the highs and lows.

The first ten chapters were originally written jointly with the character known as Just Maybe but eventually we went our separate ways and so I removed his writing.

At times it may seem disjointed but then this is not meant to be a fluent literary work instead it is an accurate record of a period of time in my life. In between writing, normal daily events took place when the writing took second, third or fourth place.

I have changed names to protect identities but all the circumstances and feelings were true at the time.

I dedicate this book to Trevor who wouldn't settle for ordinary, who helped me start my journey, and QP who encouraged me all the way but eventually followed his own path

Chapter One

It's a sunny morning and all the snow has melted.

The night that Brian came it had snowed so much that at 9.15 I thought he wouldn't come. He did but it confirmed that he wasn't Mr Amazing. In fact my fantasy of 'doing it' with a younger man (12 years younger) was a total disappointment. I should have known when he was more interested in bringing his clothes out of the car rather than swooping me into his arms and when he needed to look up the score of his team on Teletext. But I was new to this, a totally inexperienced woman with only two blokes in the last 30 years. I didn't know the etiquette of dating. When was it the right time to jump someone or let them jump me? I had a complete gap in my education and was trying my best to have a quick refresher course.

It had snowed the first night with David and that hadn't gone that brilliantly either, but this time I knew that I hadn't met Mr Amazing. Well, actually I knew that before we met up for the pub, curry and smooch on the settee.

So here I was, Mrs much-more-heavy-than Bridget Jones, 47 years old, with two pre-teen kids, wondering what the heck I was doing and frankly feeling a bit like a tart.

The next day I rang Mike, he was so nice about it. You see it could have been Brian or Mike – I just couldn't choose, they were so different – but Mike was always so busy that meeting up with him seemed to be in the distant future. He said I shouldn't worry and I suppose I didn't because I just always wanted to know.

I looked at the letter I had received from Dave and decided to ring him. I left a message on his mobile and then thought you silly fool, what are you doing?

So I went to work and they all looked at me in a certain way; some asked, others pretended they weren't listening, but they all wanted to know. The jokes had flown around the team meeting of my nightly encounters with streams of men. The websites said that if you put a photo on you would get five times more responses, but I couldn't cope with the responses I already got.

I just loved getting the emails though, and was mortally disappointed if there were none from them. I especially loved getting them from Just Maybe.

I had found him on a site in December and the emails had practically flown between us. He then sent me a picture of himself and I sent some pretty awful family ones of me. I had tried to get the kids to take a sexy one of me lying by the fire but I just looked like a beached whale and then when we got a decent head and shoulders the cable from the camera to the computer just didn't want to fit.

Just Maybe was gorgeous; I swooned looking at his pic and waited in eagerness for his emails. I was sixteen again and in love and it was fantastic. But of course he didn't feel the same. He was very polite about it; he never actually said anything, he just took no interest in me, only my writing, and so I ditched his pic and the emails and decided to put him down to experience.

I suppose the experience of my life was that you don't aim at dishy - looking blokes, not someone like me. Of course, I knew that on the flirting charts I could win hands down but I'd have to keep them away from my photograph as long as I could.

I had been doing this since November but hadn't really found anyone that exciting until December except for Just Maybe, and if this was a film then obviously the outcome would be that after all the trials and tribulations he would just know he was madly in love with me and want to be a true father to my kids. Of course it wasn't and he wouldn't. No, I'd just have to accept that it wasn't meant to be, but why some of those men put their photographs on I really didn't know. They might be very nice people inside but I just flicked past them and of course I feared that is what they would do with me.

Chapter Two

The fire was roaring at last. It had taken quite a long time to get going tonight. I knew that I should have stoked it up before I took Phoebe and Josh to their singing lesson. I don't begrudge being a mum but sometimes I wish that there were more things just for me.

I suppose that is why I was so vulnerable. When you are on your own with two young kids and an imagination like mine what do you do? I hadn't really done much with the internet – I was a social worker, not a computer person – and I had found there was nothing of great interest to me. Everyone said that you could find lots of stuff. Well, where was it then, because I couldn't?

I suppose I first went in the chat room out of nosiness. I'd heard about them but never ventured in.

My modem had been broken for several months but now it was working again, and one day I found David. He went under the name of Ramses and I had picked Isissun for my name so I thought well it must be fate, two Egyptian names together.

The fire was roaring nicely and I was pushed back into reality and the present.

I had been on the date with Brian and it just hadn't been as good as David. I had been so passionately in love with David; he was in my thoughts all the time, and when I finally found out the truth of what I suspected all along – that he had been cheating on me – I just had to do something to get him out of my mind.

So I wasted a whole load of money by ringing up psychics.

Some of the things they said were revealing and calming; other things were downright ridiculous. I began to think that, just like Gamblers Anonymous, I would have to join Psychics Anonymous because I was getting addicted and the financial costs were enormous.

One night I even rang a witch and asked her to perform a spell to get David out of my head. It was a great experience and for millionaires with nothing else to spend their money on it's highly recommended, the ultimate in relaxation.

Then, one day, I bought one of those woman mystical magazines and instead of ringing the psychic I wrote to the dating site for people who cared about their environment. I waited excitedly for a reply and found a few days later that my profile wouldn't be included for about a month, but they had an online site too. So I found the site and was pleased with my technical skills when I actually managed to join. On the site were profiles and you could email prospective dates. I picked a few men aged between 39 and 52 because I'd rather go for younger men than older.

Over the next couple of days I had a few 'hello' emails. Some I followed up, others I tried to avoid because they contained eloquent essays of how they achieved perfect ecology or how they had auditioned for the latest amateur operatic society presentation. All jolly nice, I thought, and probably terribly nice and affectionate men, but not for me. I wanted wild, unusual, daring. I knew that underneath my natural shy attire I could be erotic, flirtatious and sufficiently wacky to attract the attention of many men who wouldn't give me a second look in the street.

And then one day I found him, Clive the Hack, and I started my most exciting adventure for many years.

Chapter Three

I hadn't seen Clive the first time around through the trawl of profiles. Some of them were so long and so the same that I wanted to reply and say, "rewrite please", but then perhaps not everyone is impatient like me. I am great at new ideas but just get too damned impatient. I suppose the awful thing is I see myself in Josh and it's an awful trait. So when I sent the hello email to Clive I wanted a response straight away.

Of course I had lots of things that I should have been doing in my mumsey role, but I'm the wacky mum who does mad things, not the everything-is-beautifully-presented mum. I often wish that I could be one of those women who has everything wonderfully organised and cleans the windows on a regular basis as well as keeping everywhere and everyone tidy and spick and span.

But I'm not. I'm the mum that says at 8am on a sunny day when the kids are sprawled out in front of the telly watching kinder-long-a-pop something splurged with cartoon things hiding under the blanket, 'Let's go to Aberdovey'. And after putting up with the moans and groans I manage to get all three of us out the door in 43 minutes and off we go in a haze of grumps drowned by the latest pop CD that Josh has conned me into buying.

Yes that's me, wacky. I am so reassured when Mike says wacky is great.

So the email went and I did get distracted strangely enough. It was a Sunday night and I think that there was actually something decent on TV, and of course Phoebe had forgotten to do her homework.

So Monday came and I looked for my mobile. I do remember occasionally to take it with me in case school rings or the car breaks down. There was a message which said that I had received an email from Clive. I was so excited. You see, Clive is a journalist and it has always been my ultimate dream to live with a fellow writer; someone who could enter my dream-world with me and tune into my thoughts.

So within two minutes I found myself married to Clive, totally adored by him for ever and ever and never to be lonely ever again.

You see reading is nice but dreaming and writing is ace.

I switched the computer on and for the thousandth time wondered why the internet connection made such laboured grating sounds and there was the email from Clive; and the start of the most wonderfully exciting three days and a complete distraction from David.

I did the housewifely things and mumsey things and got under the duvet with Josh for our nightly chat and cuddle but the thrill and kicks for that brief time came from the texts and emails from Clive. He wanted to meet up and although I was a bit reserved about this and wondered who I could get to look after the kids, I agreed.

Monday and Tuesday had passion and bawd thrown between us. Tuesday night was the long chat on the phone scheming how to meet up, and then on Wednesday it all went quiet.

Clive eventually sent a text to say that there was an important email waiting for me. So I read it and sure enough it was the back-out clause disguised as getting back with the ex who had been previously described as the woman from hell.

I took a deep breath and thought, 'saved'. I suppose I hadn't really wanted to meet Clive especially when I found out what a moody person he was but it was also so exciting and different to my everyday existence.

Eventually, after a few more days, Clive said that he couldn't text or email any more in case his ex found out. A good excuse, I thought; why couldn't he just be truthful? I'm going to make a sweeping statement that will make half the male population scream, but honesty is a female trait.

I thought of Just Maybe and whether the two women he is interested in know about each other and that he is interested in both of them. After my experience with David's deceit I decided to have an open policy, and so Mike knew about Brian and Brian knew about Mike. I knew it was a big risk and I could have ended up with neither of them, but in truth I just can't lie.

The greatest legacy from my encounter with Clive was seeking amazing. Clive had said in his profile that he wasn't looking for ordinary, he was looking for amazing; of course when I replied to him I just had to be amazing, and I suppose for two days I was.

Chapter Four

One thing that drives me up the wall is not knowing whether I am menopausal or not. As half my bed is empty or covered in junk I don't get the night sweats that I used to get when David was lying next to me but I do get the sleeplessness and I have often been known to send emails to people at 4am. I try to avoid sending text messages as I found that some blokes actually take their mobiles to bed with them.

Another annoying thing is that I wake myself with a thought or an idea which I have to write down, so I get up and roam around for a while writing down my thoughts and then return to bed, only to have to get up an hour later to get Phoebe up and off to school.

Being a lone mother can be tough but contemplating another man in your life is both exciting and scary. What I am not is a secretive person, and so as I drifted through the various men that took my fancy I found myself particularly drawn to two Mikes; one was Mike, 44 who lived about twenty miles from me and the other was Just Maybe, who turned out to be another Mike who was also 44. So I told them about each other.

What I have found during my journeys through the dating sites is that there are an awful lot of 44-year-old men seeking new women. There was also an amazing amount of men who had been married for 16 years. I wondered why no one had come up with a theory about the patterns.

I'm not sure whether it was Mike 44 or Just Maybe 44 that I

found first and I suppose that has been the main irritation about my journey, that I have done most of the finding. Perhaps I should have put a photograph on my website profile, but if I had would they have picked me? As a woman with an imagination as sparkling as a starry sky but a conscience driven by my introverted upbringing, I would regard myself as ordinary looking, whatever that means.

If beauty was truly about the mind, then I would win every time and the whole male population would be so in love with me that I would feel suffocated and not able to breathe. But then if my mum was reading this she would say that I was just right. All through my childhood I was just right but being just right was not going to capture the heart of Just Maybe.

Of course when he listed the profile of women that would make up his soulmate I knew who some were but not others. Mike 44 was different. He seemed happy to just take me as I was, but he was fairly traditional in his approach to dating. He wasn't as exciting as Just Maybe. I got photographs of both sent to me and both were good looking. I told Mike 44 that he should smile, but I didn't tell Just Maybe that he should take his sunglasses off and fasten his shirt buttons up.

Mind you, although the two Mikes dominated the email scene there were others too. In fact there were so many I couldn't keep a track of who they all were.

You see I was good at picking a name and sending an email which aimed at the name or part of the profile rather than just saying hello. And the thing was that all of these men absolutely loved my brazen approach. They liked the strong woman but after a few days I would not hear from them any more.

As well as the two Mikes there was also Pedders; now his photograph was gorgeous and after a few emails he asked if he could ring me. He wanted a specific time to ring, which we agreed to; I made sure that I had gone to the toilet and at the right time the phone rang.

Now having been a shy, quiet child I have tried to make up for this in the last few years, and if not kept busy at work I can drive my fellow workers mad. So when Pedders said after two minutes that I didn't say much and said goodbye, I was taken aback, but found myself in fits of giggles.

Of course, Scott at work just couldn't believe this had happened. 'What?' he said. 'You had nothing to say?'

I suppose perhaps one difference between men and women is that we women often share experiences like the dating scene with our workmates. Mike 44 didn't seem to do this. He was a Brummy like me and so far had been the dominant person in my dating life. When Just Maybe decided to ditch me (as my kids would describe it) he told me to go out with Mike, and I will but I haven't yet.

Mike is most women's dream man; he is tall at 6ft 2ins, has dark hair, is slim and, from the photo, good looking, and his loyalty is overwhelming. He has stuck with me through all my flirtations for six weeks. He also has the most wonderful sense of humour.

One night during our regular Sunday chat I told him that I was wearing my dressing gown with nothing else on. He thought this was thrilling and said that it kept him excited all week. Since then he has called me Mrs No Knickers.

Yes, Mike 44 was fun but he wasn't as exciting as Just Maybe. But one day the most awful, embarrassing thing that could have happened, happened. I sent the email that was meant for Just Maybe to Mike 44.

Chapter Five

I was so ashamed of myself; how could I send that email? And what was worse was that it was a rather naughty, suggestive email. I cringed with embarrassment and thought that's it; I'll never hear from Mike 44 again. I did but, and not surprisingly perhaps, his email showed confusion.

At this point Mike and I hadn't talked on the phone, and so it was hard explaining myself; I just dug a hole and it got deeper and deeper...

Why didn't I just forget it? Well, I was new and naïve but overwhelmingly honest. I'd been on the dating scene for about a month and still thought of David all of the time. I didn't want him back but I had perpetual reminders of him being with her, the other woman, the trollop from hell. At bedtime I would think of him cuddled up with her and, frankly, be crushingly jealous. But when I saw him I saw how unhappy he was, and I didn't want to be like that.

Whether that was why I went over the top, whether it was my imagination or whether it was just some of the Christmas spirit I don't know, but I cringe now at the thought of my overtures to Just Maybe.

Yes, I went over the top. I offered him a life with me where he could concentrate on his writing. It seemed such a fabulous idea at the time and my idea of heaven to go to bed and wake up with another writer; someone to bounce ideas and themes around with. Someone who was always around to talk to, to go for walks with. Yes it was my heaven but it wasn't his and he told me to go out with Mike 44 and of course I decided not to.

I asked him what he expected when he sent me his photo (a different one) and a piece of music that he had composed. And so I destroyed all of his emails and the photographs and the music and put it down to experience, and then a few days later I regretted it because I could at least have had a happy memory of those wonderful days and swooned again at his picture.

Chapter Six

After David left I said to the children that we would decorate the study, which had been his secret domain, and turn it into a kids' room where they could hang out with their mates.

I am by no means the perfect housewife. I would much rather write a story than get out the vacuum cleaner, but the house was getting somewhat inexcusable, even for my standards. I thought if they had their room, then we could at least try to keep the living room reasonably decent so, after removing all the junk, we started dismantling the many shelves and put them in piles ready to paint. The study, kitchen and dining room all became painting shelf territories with newspaper spread everywhere, and we started to paint.

One afternoon, in the midst of a good painting session, the phone rang and one of the kids answered it. Their participation in the task was sporadic anyway. Phoebe aspires to being Princess Phoebe with an entourage of servants to please her. Josh for a change was doing ok.

'Mum... there's a bloke on the phone for you'

'Who is it?' I asked

'I don't know'.

So I wiped my hands as much as I could and spoke to the strange man on the phone. He said that he was Brian from *Natural Friends* magazine and he had seen me in the latest edition, and would I like to have a chat. I told him that I was at a crucial stage in the painting and could I ring him in an hour; he said that would be ok.

So I rang him back and I found out that he was 36 years old, although in fact he was 35; perhaps he thought 11 years difference in age sounded better than 12. I immediately said I thought I was too old for him but he said that he had lots of friends in their 40s and in fact he had been out with two women in their early 40s already.

Now one thing I could never understand is women who are attracted to older men; the thought of having a relationship with a 59 year old just totally turns me off.

I began to think about my own requirements and realised how I was really quite prejudiced; for example I knew from a previous experience I liked men to be taller than me. I would rather have someone 6ft 2in (like Mike 44) than even an inch smaller than me.

I also wanted them if not to have a decent job, to have a passion in life that makes them sparkle and buzz. Of course I wanted me to be part of their buzz but I didn't want to be all-consuming like I had been at the beginning for David. It had isolated me from my friends and had made me ultimately lonely.

And Brian was interested in me; I turned him on and he turned me on too. But like all the men I have met so far it wasn't enough.

I had loved the wonderful to-ing and fro-ing between me and Clive and when Just Maybe lavished the same attention on me I grabbed it with both hands.

Brian rang about every four days and I rang him. I find it so hard to not be in touch with someone I fancy and if they don't ring me I think they can't really like me. But there was something different about Brian and there was the added bonus he was so much younger. Most of the women I know would love the chance of being admired by a younger man and those that I told were thrilled for me. Especially a younger man who was single, had no kids and wasn't bothered about having any, had a brain in his head and a decent job.

Now the decent job bit for me was only so they didn't become financially dependent on me, because through my husband's death I had enough for me to work part time and keep me and the kids afloat. So I was 47 and past my child-bearing years, with a nice house, two interesting kids and enough money to get by, so all that was missing was a bloke for the other things in life.

The trouble was that I just couldn't choose between Mike 44 and Brian. They were so different and of course every so often I would think of Just Maybe, but then I soon realised that was a dead end. He would never be interested in me. He was seeking his dolly bird – misguidedly, I thought – but as time went on and more blokes rumbled past me his appeal became less and less.

But he did come back to me. I had a sneaky feeling he would; not because he fancied me but because he liked my writing. It wasn't like his but he liked it and that was fine by me.

So for three weeks I talked to both Brian and Mike 44 on the phone and one day or hour I would favour one and the next the other.

When I had first talked to David I had said that I really need-ed three men for different roles in life and I'll leave those roles to your imagination. Suddenly I found these men emerging because not only were there Mike 44, Brian and Just Maybe, there was also Happy Dog with a prospect of a fling on my holiday in Spain, and there was Knightly, who I'd written to as his Emma and who had been so thrilled that at last someone had recognised his disguise.

I had talked about going to stay with him to attend the Jane Austen Society AGM with his two gay friends. Our emails were very supportive of each other until he started along a bawdy route which was rather seedy and didn't represent our relationship, and so I just let the emails fizzle out.

And then there was the ecology group chat room.

Chapter Seven

Every night at about 11pm there are a small group of people who meet up in a chat room. They all belong to a site which is aimed at people who care about their environment. They are all non-smokers and many are vegetarians.

This was the first site that I went on and, after scanning the profiles of members, I found many were similar and too long-winded. I found the chat room and I became a regular visitor.

Now I had been in the large free public chat rooms under the category of 40s' romance and had occasionally found someone interesting to chat with amongst the general bawd and filth but they were usually living in the states and so the chances of getting to know them beyond the chat room was minimal.

I had no intention of moving anywhere. My kids come first and they are happy and settled here. The problem with David and me was that with him living 200 miles away it meant that we either had to go for it, and we did, or have this occasional relationship which neither of us could cope with.

David was all-consuming and I missed that but I also realised that perhaps it was the wrong time to seek amazing. My kids were too young to go it alone and so I knew whoever I spent time with would have to accept that this was the case.

My mum was 82 years old and although pretty fit might need more of my attention over the next few years. So I thought perhaps I should settle for Mr Nice. Now that doesn't mean that Mr Nice might not turn out to be Mr Amazing but I suppose I always thought that Mr Amazing would just hit me for six one day. I was such a romantic at heart.

I had spent so much of my time with Tim on my own and for the last three years of our marriage he had worked away during the week and at weekends he spent very little time with me and the kids because of the major work needing doing to the house.

This time around I wanted someone who would want to and be able to spend a lot of time with me. I had always been a very accommodating woman and was very loving. I was also fun and wacky and so once I found him I felt that there was no problem in charming him and being a romantic; it was easy to fall in love. But I suppose this time around there were so many things that I wanted, including the prospect of someone who liked sex as much as me.

I can remember when I was Phoebe's age the idea of someone my age having sex was seen as awful; she feels much the same. But I just love that level of closeness.

When I was in my late teens I worked with some women in their late 30s and they used to talk about sex a lot and how it was a trial. So many of them lived with men that they really didn't like very much.

I now looked at family and friends and so many of them didn't have their Mr Amazing. Sometimes I was jealous and thought it would be nice to live with Mr OK but I thought 'Why?' I don't need to and I realised that a lot of my problem was actually living with myself. It was hard living with myself; there were so many times when myself wasn't enough and even though I adored my children there were days when I thought how nice it would be just to be able to go out and seek Mr Amazing.

I always joked that I could be standing next to him in the supermarket or he could be the next social worker that I met when I changed jobs. But what were the chances of that? I looked at the men in the supermarket and thought 'I wonder who you are and whether you have your Amazing?'

But then I was too shy, oh yes I could chat in the queue but that was all.

And I found myself in the chat room and found the four regulars that came in every night and I joined in the chat and they welcomed me and it was a comfort to my loneliness and let the evening become the night, but when we all said our goodbyes I went up to bed alone and filled up my water bottle, feeling OK about life but wishing I could trade my water bottle for a hot man.

Chapter Eight

I told you how I tinkered with a few psychics. Well, I decided to
do the same with the dating sites. The chat room was nice to be
in just before bedtime but during the day there was nothing
going on there. I suppose that I should have been getting on with
life and doing the gardening or washing the windows or sorting
out those boxes that have the same junk in them that has been
there for the last year but that you just can't seem to get yourself
to throw away . Nobody has used anything for ages but you never
know. And the odd socks pile with so many of the same, but not
quite the same, coloured socks.

Yes, I should have kept myself busy doing tasks like that but I
didn't, I sought out two more sites.

One of the sites had profiles and at the end of the profile it
matched you to the person's star sign. Of course, I then learned
which of the star signs was supposed to be the best match for me
and went through the search for the men aged 39 to 52 who
matched that star sign.

The emails trickled through and at times flooded through and
I politely discarded the smokers, who usually sent a message
through saying it was my loss and I thought, 'Oh no it isn't; not if
you have an attitude like that it isn't.'

Also so many of the profiles were boring I found myself changing my profile and my name.' I couldn't just be Rachel 202 that
was too boring and so I picked some kind of romantic or explicit
names. It was fun changing my names.

Just Maybe came along after the first change. I had started as Your Future and became The Story Teller. I am currently Magic Carpet but by the time you read this I will probably have had six more names.

Yes, it was nice to match with the star signs and to dream that one of these people might actually be Mr Amazing. One of the other things about the site is that you could choose your favourites and you had your admirers.

One day I found a new admirer but I won't mention his name.

I sent him an email because he fitted my bill and was a published writer. So we emailed and then after a brief time we talked on the phone. He had his own website, which was of a political nature and I suppose – given the time to look at it properly – would have been quite interesting. But at that time I was quite busy at work, with kids' activities, and had a flood of emails coming in.

So I chatted to him. I had told him about writing my autobiography and why I was doing it and he sent me an email saying how difficult it was to publish and that publishers would only publish celebrity's autobiographies. I knew all that and that was why I felt that it was important; I had planned to use some of the money I had inherited from Tim to pay for this. But it was his attitude, he was so arrogant. I spoke to him on the phone and he patronised me and kept calling me dear.

Well, most people would just have ignored it but I felt that there had been lots of times in my life when I had been really downtrodden and this time I wasn't going to put up with it. So I rang him up and got his answerphone, which I was glad of, and left him a message to say how arrogant I thought he was and how that very day a publisher had asked me for a synopsis of my book.

He was what people warn you of, but I suppose in lots of ways he was harmless. People who don't go online wonder why you do;

they tell you to go and join a group. That's easier said than done. First you have to join a group that is interesting but then the chances are that the available men there, and especially the ones which fit your spec, number nil, and don't forget you also have to find the childminder at the appropriate cost to look after the kids, who play them up anyhow.

I have found the attitudes of outsiders fall into two camps: those that are a little bit jealous and would like to try it themselves but haven't got the nerve; and those who are so strongly against that they make you feel that you are carrying out an immoral act. I suppose at times I feel the same but I have and am enjoying my time. Perhaps it is because I am a social worker but there are some very interesting people with their stories to tell and, being a storyteller too, it's nice to share them with you.

My urgency to find Mr Amazing waxes and wanes. In fact, having two men that liked me made me terribly indecisive. I just didn't want to hurt either of them. It was fortunate that the decision was made for me. Mike 44 was too busy at work. I was having a Chinese New Year Party and had asked him to come but that weekend he was going to visit his brother. His work was so hectic and he was so tired from trips all around the country that no time was right. I began to think that he didn't really like me but I suppose I knew he really did. Anyhow Brian said, 'Let's meet', and the decision was made. I would meet him by the clock tower in the Market Square on Friday at eight o'clock.

Chapter Nine

The day I met Brian I also reached my personal high or, if you know Maslow's Hierarchy of needs, Self Actualisation. Everything was going my way that day.

I had a letter in the post to say that I had won £10,000, had an email from the publisher to say that they were going to consider my book, *The Nameless Social Worker* and I was on my way to meet with Brian. The older woman's dream meeting with the younger man. I didn't know what Brian looked like. I only had a rough description, but I liked his Welsh accent, especially the way he talked about ringing his 'cronies'.

So I drove to Stafford and I was high as a kite. The only problem I had was the most god awful menopausal period. So the chances of jumping each other were a definite no no.

You men are so lucky; the only way you can naturally embarrass yourself is by nicking your chins in a sloppy shaving session. Us late 40s menopausal women not only have to feel the need for gallons of evening primrose but also have to consider should we have a hysterectomy like our mothers. All those adverts showing the woman in her white trousers... well look how old she is?

So I arrived to meet Brian wearing a darkish skirt and felt so out of place amongst the uniform of young black trouser-wearers. I had looked for something new to wear, partly to treat myself, but everything in the shops seemed so dreary and it was all green and brown. When you have worn your brothers cast-offs as a child, which were green and brown you naturally steer away from those colours.

So I drove to Stafford and now I reveal another secret; well, it isn't really but I haven't mentioned it before. I just adore singing at the top of my voice in the car, and especially to ABBA. There is nothing better than pretending that you are the kid who kissed the teacher. Of course, the dancing queen is great too but I haven't got it on this particular CD.

The kids and I have this fab game, which we play with new-to-the-car-kids. When we get half a mile out of our village, suddenly I will drive like a racing driver, put the radio or a CD on full blast and open all the windows. They love it and I do too.

But today it was ABBA and on the way to meet Brian. Of course I realised I was high as a kite so at the traffic lights and the speed camera I had to sober myself up and become a bit more nicely demure. I had no intention of putting him off straight away. We had agreed to go to a pub and then have a meal and see what went from there. I said I'd treat him so there was no awkwardness. I am a modern woman and so don't expect men to pay for me. Perhaps I also like to be in the power position too.

I walked up to the clock tower and saw this man waiting for me and I thought, 'Blimey, he's good looking', and he was. I gave him a hug and then we walked to a pub that I had never been in but seemed a bit more fun. Brian bought me a drink but the only place we could sit was by the dart board. So we sat and chatted and it felt OK, although I was a bit motherish, telling him off for biting his nails.

His eye contact wasn't as good as mine so I looked away a bit too. I didn't feel at all scared. No, I was quite comfortable with Brian. So we had one drink and then we decided to go and look for somewhere to eat. We settled on an Indian. We got up to leave and of course I did the mandatory knocking of the bowl of chalks onto the floor.

Brian was a total gentleman and, being the super-conservationist that he is, was immediately down on the floor picking them up. It was a gem and I just giggled and I suppose it put him more at his ease. I was also able to get my first really close-up look and, wow, Brian had the most gorgeous skin for a bloke and I thought how enjoyable my compromising position was. I suddenly had one of those chemical surges.

Chapter Ten

We walked along to the Indian restaurant, walked in and were faced by a rather grouchy-looking elderly waiter. This gave me even more giggles and helped Brian relax even more.

Usually I like the full works–starter, main meal and pud–but on this occasion neither Brian or I were starving so we settled for the main meals, having a bit of each other's and the glass of lager to swig it down with.

I can be an elegant, genteel lady when I feel it's appropriate. Brian was nice and easy going and quite a catch for the right girl so I suppose I wondered what on earth he was doing with me. He knew nothing about me having any money and had a decent job himself, so I found it totally flattering that he just fancied me as I was.

So we ate the meal and then it seemed rather tacky just to go to another pub in Stafford and so we decided to go back to my village, dump the cars and walk to a local pub. So Brian followed me.

When we got to the house I said I would have to pop in for two mins to see the kids otherwise they would wonder why the car was there. I asked him whether he wanted to say hello or not. He said he did and Josh took me aside and said, 'Hey Mum, he's good looking.'

I felt a bit like a woman in a film who brings a stream of blokes home as Uncle so and so. Which just showed that I was not very good at this game.

We went to the pub and then walked back to the house. By now the chemicals were at full speed, spreading around my body. As I walked along the road I wanted to hold Brian's hand but instead pushed my arm through his. Initially he didn't seem happy with this and so I took it away and told him that he didn't seem happy. He said that he did and so I put it back. His grip was firm and felt safe.

Back at the house the children were still roaming around, which was not the most conducive thing for romantic overtures but I soon managed to get them to bed.

We sat on the settee and I decided not to do anything. Brian leant over and kissed me and then I just wished...

Chapter Eleven

Brian and I tried to work out when we could meet up again. We knew that just a meal in a pub wasn't enough and I was wary of what the kids would think but I just had to know what it was like with a man 12 years my junior.

I decided to be reasonably open about it and told my mum that I planned to have Brian stay over. He couldn't arrive until late so the children wouldn't see him anyhow. Mum talked about my reputation and I laughed as Brian would be only the third man in 30 years. How many other women could claim to be that squeaky clean. But I know what she meant and if he had lived twenty rather than seventy miles away it could have been easier.

So the plot was set and I waited for Brian to arrive and, of course, it snowed and it got to 9.30pm and I waited for the phone call to say that he wasn't coming and he nearly turned back. He arrived and he made the first, biggest blunder that he could. He went in the boot of his car to get out his clothes for the next day and I felt that we had been married for ten years, not that it was a clandestine romantic interlude.

I wanted him to come in and sweep me off my feet but no... he walked in carrying his clothes and I couldn't help compare it to the time when David had decided to drive 200 miles to come and see me on a whim, only to have to drive back for work six hours later. Yes, I am an old romantic at heart.

So that was a bad start and when we had the teletext football scores on and the persistent request to set the alarm for some god awful early hour it just made the rest of it Okish.

So the next day I felt like a tart, just as my mum had said, and that evening rang up Mike 44.

He laughed and told me that I shouldn't worry. I said that I didn't think I wanted to see Brian again and that I should have been more patient and waited for Mike. He said we will meet anyhow and that I would always have wanted to know what it was like. Mike is so wise and I wished that I could be just like him but I'm not and he wouldn't want me to be.

The day before I met Brian I coincidentally had emails from all of my male acquaintances. Some knew I was going on a date, others were just catching up. It felt as though they were all there looking after me. And so I had to tell them how it had gone.

The thing was I really liked Brian and I still do but like is the optimum word. I had been swept away by all sorts of feelings the majority of which now I think were feelings of flattery, that someone his age who was good looking, had a brain and a decent job should be interested in me. I would love to stay friends but how do you? Mike would say things will be what they are meant to be.

Chapter Twelve

I suppose, before I went on the dating sites I regarded myself as a failure. I should have been able to meet a decent man just in my ordinary life but when you work primarily with women and don't have a huge social life your chances are pretty limited. I suppose also that even up until now if I am truly honest it has been hard getting over David, I know that Just Maybe has felt the same about getting over Lisa. If you have truly loved someone the way I did David and Just Maybe did Lisa, then you have permanent reminders and comparisons.

The other thing that I have found is that I will be completely honest with men. I don't want that deception ever again and just won't tolerate it; I won't deceive anyone in that way. Although I am truly friends with David and probably always will be, I hate him for his deception and I cannot understand how Jenny wants someone like him. How could she ever trust him. How can she ever know that he isn't screwing every woman that he comes across and that he isn't spending time with me like he was with her. No, I just can't understand it and I understand it even less when she, like me, met David from a chat room and so knows the amount of lonely men that there are just waiting for someone. Of course, whoever gets me gets the crème de la crème so perhaps that's why Mike 44 hangs in there for me lol (as they say on the net).

I have and continue to meet some very interesting men on the net. I say men because you tend, unless you are gay I suppose, to meet people from the opposite sex and I suppose, because this book is all about seeking amazing and about the experience of a heterosexual person, that it gives a one-sided view. I know very little about the women that come on the sites because I generally only chat with the men. Although, on the chat room I go in, it is men and women and occasionally I talk privately to the women.

I am also like Just Maybe, selective about the men I chat to. I have decided now only to talk to non-smokers, mostly to men with no kids and of medium to slim build, who do something interesting workwise and, of course, are significantly taller than me. I suppose, like everyone else, if I see someone without a pic I am more likely to chat with them rather than with someone who I don't fancy.

One of the things I find intriguing is the site that has the whispers (where you can chat directly to a chosen person); it times all of your chats and so, when you are waiting for a reply sometimes there has only been a minute delay and yet it seems like ages. I recently looked back at how many people I had talked to over the last three months and I have lost count. On one of the sites I currently have seventeen admirers and yet some of them have never sent me an email.

As well as Brian, I have a number of younger men who have put me on their list and I have a chap, another published writer much younger than me, who is sending me quite a few emails.

It is all a very interesting experience and I suppose 'interesting', in lots of ways, is the right word because no one hits me as amazing. But is amazing like hitting gold?

But, like Just Maybe, I am impatient.

Of course I would have really liked to have fallen madly in love with him but what would then have happened if he too, like Brian, was more interested in what he was going to wear the next day and being at work on time rather than the excitement of being with me. But then I know that, like me, he'd go for the excitement and have a great charming apology for being late at work.

Yes, Just Maybe could have been my Mr Amazing but he chose, like Mr Darcy, to condemn me and to send me the Dear John letter. But what he didn't realise at the time was that, just like in *Pride and Prejudice*, I am very like Elizabeth Bennet.

Chapter Thirteen

I finished rinsing through the socks and knickers and wondered why, when I had packed, it always seemed so many but then was never enough.

The children had gone to play table tennis. They were friends now and in a world of their own.

I looked out towards the sea and saw a glistening light, it was so much better today. The wind howled but I found it a comforting noise. The sun shone and made the Nerja mountains seem suddenly dramatic. The howling wind and the waves seemed to be talking to each other.

When I lay in the sun, the wind blew hard and I felt cold but when the sun came out I felt exhilarated. It felt so good, I felt so beautiful but then I looked at myself in the bath and thought no wonder I was alone. How could anyone love that body, that joke of a body which was concealed for most of the time by an array of clothes.

I knew that there were far worse bodies than mine. I had seen them displayed in the dining room but it was my body and I had no excuse for the way that I was.

The sun was shining brightly and I thought of the men back home, the ones I had enchanted by my emails and entranced by my magical tones on the telephone, if only they knew the truth that this woman who could capture their hearts was just one big fake. I was no beauty, but then had I ever pretended to be.

I accepted people as they are, but then did I? I too was

entranced by beauty. I too wanted, just once in my life, to be loved by the gorgeous man. The complete man, the one whose body and soul were truly beautiful. But then I thought as I looked around the dining room at the couples whose days were numbered, had they sought that beauty too. Had any of them found it?

I thought of the men on the dating site seeking slim and attractive. Was that enough or, when they found it, would they add so many requirements to the list that that woman could never be found?

The wind continued to howl and I wondered whether he, Mr Slim and Beautiful, would love the wind as I did. Would he see the patterns in the clouds? Would he love to sing with me and to me? Would he watch as I wrote in my imagination pad? I didn't know but it was nice dreaming that he would.

I sat curled up on one of the two settees, looked out at the blue sky with the floating clouds and had a warm feeling, a feeling of excitement, a feeling of anticipation.

Chapter Fourteen

I suppose the idea of writing a book with a stranger was just terribly exciting and a challenge especially with someone I had made such a fool of myself with by offering him my world. If he had accepted it I imagine I would have freaked out. You see, one of the joys of being a writer is that you can be whoever you want to be and, with an imagination like mine, I could certainly do that. But with Just Maybe I had to tell the blatant truth. I had been entranced by his writing, although I thought, 'Why doesn't he write the real story stories? Things about his own life. He obviously likes history because he sets his stories in times gone by rather than now? I thought he must have a fabulous story to tell about his unrequited love.

Is it just him or is it him being part of the male species that means he doesn't dare tell another soul, let alone perhaps several million, about his heart, about his pain, about his loss?

I wondered about these things and why it was that I was willing to tell. Was it because I was a woman or was it just me?

I hadn't met Just Maybe and was more determined than ever that we shouldn't meet but surely I wanted to meet him just to know for certain that what he said was true, that as well as me not being his Ms Amazing that he wasn't my Mr Amazing.

Could it be that he could be my unrequited love? I didn't think so but we did have some purpose.

Would we be like Gilbert and Sullivan – write well together but despise each other?

I thought about love and how it was so easy to love people and in so many different ways. I did feel a kind of love for Just Maybe, but it wasn't what I felt for David or what I was beginning to feel for Mike 44. As I was here in Nerja I so missed his texts and our occasional chats on the phone. But I didn't miss Just Maybe because as I wrote I felt this distant connection knowing that he too was writing. The book was our connection, our link and it satisfied a need which was a common part of both of us.

I thought of how I had lost the urge to write during the first few days in Spain. It was as if I had left it all behind in England with Just Maybe. But when I visited the Nerja caves on 20th February 2003 my urge to write had come soaring back. I wondered whether Just Maybe was writing back home in England.

The Nerja caves had been my inspiration, they were so wonderful, so inspiring. As I walked in the caves my desire to write came back in full force and I realised that, as well as the topic, I needed the venue to write. I also began to realise that seeking amazing was not just about that close connection with a particular man, it was about a whole experience.

I had felt constrained in the hotel. We were told that our lucky dip of three hotels had landed us with the best, but two mornings of being woken in the early hours by the Nerja dustmen had not been our treat. So I had complained and we moved rooms to the suite with the two camp beds; of course, Josh managed to break the one I was to sleep on in one minute flat, jumping on it.

I responded by being the typical grouchy mother who went into a sulk. He and, Phoebe suddenly became the greatest pals and set to proving that they had their fathers talent for mending things. And when later the maid, cleaner or whatever you call them broke the bed again they proved their case.

Now it was 1.30am and I had dreamed of a one-eyed ugly person who was supposed to be my Mr Amazing and I awoke thinking of the three key men in my life David, Just Maybe and Mike 44.

Just Maybe said how dreadful he looked in the morning. Looks seemed to play an awful part in his life. He had admitted to placing a younger pic in his second profile and I suppose I had fallen for it as I had sent him an email saying I liked his pic. He didn't respond but then he was going through his Dear John phase, trying to chase me away.

I thought about Just Maybe and how exciting the fantasy was but the intriguing thing was that I could fantasise about many more fun things with Mike 44. He was the one that liked my wackiness and he was the one I so desperately wanted to meet.

I loved writing to and with Just Maybe but I thought that if we met it would spoil all the magic and I might find myself disappointed. No, I wanted to meet Mike 44. I wanted to know what it was like just seeing his 6ft 2in frame towering above me but because of what Just Maybe had said about looks and beauty I began to fear that Mike 44 would not like me.

I thought of *Bridget Jones's Diary* and how she had been fooled by instant charm and looks. But the truth was that, although I was a lot heavier than I would like to have been, I looked pretty good with my hair in knots just wearing a blue sleeveless T-shirt and a pair of knickers and the only thing that enhanced my looks was the good old Olay as I naturally have the colouring that so many women spend hours trying to achieve.

Just Maybe had talked so much about looks but I didn't know what he sounded like.

Steve had told me that Sue sounded very squeaky on the phone and he thought that was why men were put off. I had my Brummy lilt but it never really put men off, although when I talked to the self-published author he was condescending and I wondered whether it was because of my accent. People with my accent don't have professor grandfathers, do they?

He had been so patronising that when the publishers said that they were going to consider my autobiography I just wanted to stick two fingers up at him for his condescending manner. No one except him had treated me in such a way.

I knew that David was not Mr Amazing. If David had had a job just using his voice he would have made millions. I remember the mother of a friend of Josh's being very apologetic when she heard that David and I had split up, admitting that whenever she heard his voice she would swoon.

I suppose hearing Mike 44's familiar Brummy tones had initially put me off. How strange, I thought, when David had said that he loved my Brummy accent.

But now in the early hours in Spain I just so wanted to hear those Brummy tones. To get my' Morning Mrs No Knickers' email. It was only a few days but I missed it so.

'Is Mike the one?' I thought.

Chapter Fifteen

Anyone reading this book will begin to feel that, just as no one goes to the toilet in a film, I don't have a life beyond seeking amazing. Of course I do. I still have to do those mundane things like food shopping, making meals and being attentive to my children, my mother and my friends. I also go to work but am fortunate to work part time. When my husband died two years ago I inherited some money. Not enough to say I was rich but enough to pay off my mortgage and enable me to work part time.

I work as a social worker through an agency. This means that I get to work for short periods of time, usually three to six months, in different settings. I work sometimes with children and their families and sometimes with adults, which is predominantly older people. Sometimes I think it would be nice to work in the same place as I get to know my work colleagues and then move on. But my kids are the most important people to me and they like me to be around during the holidays, nowadays to be their base camp. My kids are 10 and 12, so you can see some of the difficulties I have in finding the right man because I wouldn't even contemplate someone who didn't like kids.

I suppose that's why Mike 44 was so attractive because, as well as being 6ft 2 in tall, slim and, from his photo, reasonably good looking, he has a son who is a week older than Phoebe who he spends loads of time with and even helps with homework.

My kids would say that their mum is lovely and wacky and great at making up stories and fun things to do but when it comes to helping with the homework she is pretty crap. It's a good job that both of them are fairly bright and have a network of friends to ask when they get stuck.

But I'm a good social worker and I will tackle any cause which needs fighting for. My particular interest is the relationship between social work and the media. I think that the general public are pretty ignorant about what we do, but I won't go harping on about it here. If you want to know any more, then read my other book, *The Nameless Social Worker* ... end of advert plug.

Social work can be very stressful though. Just before I went to Spain for half term I had been preparing reports for court for a child who needed a second chance. He was only two but the lack of love and stimulation he got, not just from his mum but all of his family, was minimal. One of my colleagues had described him as being treated like a dog and, in fact, she felt that a dog would probably be treated better.

Now you'd say, 'Why didn't you get him out of there then? 'Well, you see, its not that easy because she gave him food and put clothes on him and didn't leave dangerous things around but that was about it. I'm afraid that if I did that little with my kids I'd want someone to take them off me and give them a better deal in life. I suppose another difficulty for me going on a dating site is wondering why so many men are divorced. What went wrong in their relationship? Would history repeat itself with me?

I know that I am a very intense person and when I describe myself as passionate I certainly am but lots of men could probably not cope with that for any length of time.

I know that I was separated but I reckon spending over a decade living in a complete wreck of a house with the last three years having your husband work away all week leaving me with two little kids makes me feel that my seperation was justified.

I have staying power and staying in there, keeping the links between the kids and their dad was important to me.

I'm passionate about my work too. I really want the best for the people I work with. Many of them have had terrible lives and although I've had sad things happen in mine they are generally just bad luck things. I have never been abused. I would say that I was neglected by my husband when he left me all week in a wreck with two small children while he worked away but I certainly have never experienced the abuse that many adults and children I have worked with over the years receive.

I described myself as being like Elizabeth Bennet out of *Pride and Prejudice* and as Jane Austen was an observer of her society I am of ours. But I would rather have Mr Knightly, Emma's chap, than Mr Darcy. I like the straight-talking bloke who will tell me that I'm daft if he thinks it matters and I think that perhaps I have found him in Mike 44. If I could only get to meet him.

Entering the dating sites for me has been a change from watching the TV. I am not particularly a computer fan; mine gets switched on and off. It is a laptop; I like to be comfy when I chat to men. I have joked in the chat room about taking everyone to bed with me but haven't done that for a while.

What I also find intriguing is the way people on the sites vary at different times of day. I was highly amused by chatting during the day with a man whose name translated to Pond. I, of course, made the awful jokes about Bond which he didn't get but when he told me that he used the site not for dating but to keep him company, like the radio, whilst he did his work as a translator I had to laugh.

One of the sites is keeping statistical information, which it claims is available to show the trends of people coming on the site but the questions that they ask to make up the profiles only have limited replies. I find the most interesting sections are the ones in which people write about where they would go on a date. One man said that he would like to go in a barrel over Niagara Falls. I must admit that I am attracted to the more wacky ideas and yet Mike 44 was one of the men who just was straight and to the point and claimed to be nervous and new to the dating scene.

Mike 44, like me, didn't put his photo on and I suppose I picked him because he didn't live too far from me. The joke is that, although he lives about three quarters of an hour away, we haven't been able to meet up yet but in the long term it seems more promising than the three and a half hours it took to go to see David.

As well as talking to prospective Mr Amazings I also talk with people who appear nice but I would never consider as possible suitors.

Chapter Sixteen

'I hate you,' I text to David, and that's how I did feel.

Two years ago I had returned to find the letter from David's ex saying that as well as seeing me he was also seeing Jenny. The letter had made him out to be absolutely evil, which I know that he isn't, so I suppose, being a woman in love, I had tried to put it behind me. At the time David said that it would always be there to haunt us and I suppose that it was but the main reason for that was because he was seeing both of us. As I've said before I got the meal and she got the scraps until I chucked him out but she was obviously happy with the scraps.

Well, I had been back a few days and I felt so cross with David so I sent him the text. Five minutes later I got a very upset David on the phone. He knew that this was just a temporary feeling because I can never hate him. I think he's a fool and I'm glad that he's no longer my partner but I can't understand why Jenny wants him when he still wants to be in touch with me and live around the corner. Of course, outsiders think that I will have him back but David knows that that will never happen, no way, especially now that I have found the dating sites and even more so because of Mike 44.

So I had a couple of days where just everything and anything made me cry, even the window cleaner. Just Maybe seemed to be having a fab time with Raine and there was me desperate to get that call from Mike 44 but he was busy and the night he rang through, rather than responding to my texts, I had gone to bed.

I wasn't really miserable, just weepy. So, of course, I started to go over the top, sending Mike 44 texts and thought, 'Oh no, I'll chase him away.' He seems to be a man who compartmentalises his life but I know that I belong in the romance compartment because he hasn't been on the dating site for over a month now and most of the time he leaves his mobile on just in case I text him.

Well, Thursday night came and he said he would be home. I said I would phone him after Phoebe's school parents evening and picking Josh up from his theatre group. So at 9.45pm I had a lovely chat, knowing that Mike was very tired. Poor Mike must get so fed up with me so I decided I needed to do something to distract myself.

The next night I had a girls' night out – a meal at a local pub for my friend's 50th birthday party. It was nice and we had a good giggle about my experiences on the dating sites but then I walked home on my own in the rain.

I had had a nice time but that night I thought that I was the only one who had no one to go home to and I just wished that Mike had been there. I knew I couldn't do anything about it but what I could do was to try to distract myself. The next day I decided that as, romantically, I didn't want anyone but Mike and I still had nine months left on the dating sites, I would start Rachel's Gang and become an online agony aunt/ social worker to all these men on the site. Perhaps I would make some friends along the way and it would keep me busy. So I emailed my seventeen admirers and put the suggestion to them. Within a couple of hours six had emailed back saying they wanted to join my gang. I also phoned Pete who I had talked to several times on the phone from the chat room. He was madly in love with a woman who kept blowing hot and cold on him. He lived about an hour from me. I've never fancied him but thought he might make a good friend and so I said, 'Let's meet up and go for a walk.' We decided to meet the following Monday at the Knutsford services and then we'd go and mooch around some charity shops together in Knutsford. Having planned an evening watching the box as Mike had his brother staying for the weekend and I knew wouldn't be in touch unexpectedly I got a text.

It was from Simon, one of the men I'd emailed about Rachel's Gang; he said that I could ring him now if I fancied a chat. Well, it was him or the box so I thought might as well ring him. Simon answered the phone and told me about his life in Majorca and how he had to escape back to the UK as there was a bloke who had put out a death threat on him. We were having a nice mates' chat and then he said he had to go and do the washing up as he was being nagged by his mum, who he had returned to live with. He said he would ring me back in ten mins. A minute later he sent a text asking if I could send him a sexy text. I thought, 'Oh no, not one of them,' and went to bed.

The next morning I found a stream of texts giving explicit details of our text-sexual acts together. He said, 'Did I want him to ring me or email?' I sent a text back saying I was looking for non-sexual friends and I thought of Mike and just wished.

And then I received a text from Brian to say that he was back from his trip in Namibia, had had a great time but he missed me and could he see me again, no strings attached.

Chapter Seventeen

I was determined not to be in a compromising situation with Brian. I wanted Mike but thought that if I met with Brian the old chemical urges might lead me to a situation which I would later regret. I really liked Brian and wanted him as a long-term friend. He had a lot in common with my mum; they both liked bird-watching and ecological things, so I thought, as well as being nice for me, mum would get something beneficial from my friendship with Brian. He was good to talk to but I so wanted to be with Mike. So I told Brian that I had sent him an email at work as he did not have email at home. I pussyfooted around and then said, 'Well, actually I've found a woman for you and she would like to get in touch with you'.

I wondered what his reaction would be but he was fairly positive about it and said that I could give her his email address.

I said that I was willing to see him again as long as it was on a friendship basis. I told him that I had felt like a tart and he said that he understood. I wondered whether it would be possible or not. We tentatively agreed for him to come over to see me a week on Thursday but we agreed to ring each other in a few days' time. Sunday went by and after going for a nice but muddy organised walk and dealing with child things and preparing a Sunday roast, I waited for the time when I could ring Mike. We usually talked at about 9.45pm, when I knew that the kids were settled, but tonight I tried ringing earlier but found that he was on the phone.

The first time I had spoken to Mike, which seemed like a century ago, I was having an awful day with Josh. Mike had rung at around 7pm and I told him that I would have to ring back later when the kids were in bed.

Josh and I were having a terrible time together and he had become the monster child from hell. He was totally impossible and was even becoming violent towards me. I knew that it was a reaction to the male losses in his life. Tim, his dad, and Gramps, my dad, dying and David and I splitting up. I had considered paying privately for him to see a psychologist but Josh is a bright kid and would learn within a very short time how to manipulate them. No, I just had to ride the wave again but it would happen the first night I spoke to Mike. In fact, by the time I spoke to Mike that first night I was nearly in floods of tears, a great way to start a possible romance, and then, during our discussion, Josh had come down grabbed the phone off me and farted down it.

OK, it seems funny now and Mike praised Josh for his imaginative approach, understanding the stress that he was under but it was certainly touch and go at the time. But tonight, though, I just wanted to hear that voice I so looked forward to hearing.

Mike answered the phone and I just talked and talked and he listened. I didn't want to keep saying about meeting up as I knew the work pressures that Mike was under so we talked about the weekend and I told him that Brian was back. He said 'He still wants you then,' and I said that whether he did or not the only person that I wanted was Mike. There were some silences during the discussion when I would so liked to have seen Mike's face. I knew that I was trying hard to be patient and I was trying even harder not to fall in love with Mike. He said, 'How could you fall in love with someone that you have never met?' but I knew that you could because that is what happened with David. But this time I had to suppress my feelings.

Chapter Eighteen

Steve had rung me a few times and had talked about the woman he was in love with. I had met Steve in the chat room off the ecology site and we decided to phone each other. I suppose I found myself in my online social work hat and enjoyed listening to Steve's story. He also had a nice voice and I wondered what he looked like but I never fancied Steve. He sounded too like me and that sounded like a lethal combination; besides, at the time, I had the triangle of Just Maybe, who I fancied like hell, Brian and Mike – I just didn't know which I liked the best. I was also trying to sort out my feelings about David so I just couldn't handle taking on Steve as well. He was in love anyhow and was looking for a younger woman to have kids with and so this time I could be just friends.

Steve seemed fed up the last time I had spoken to him and so I had suggested that we meet up and go for a walk. We decided to meet on the Monday and go into Knutsford, mooch around the charity shops and then go for a walk.

Of course, as usual, I wasn't very prepared and although I had given myself enough time I hadn't looked which junction I should take off the M6 so I went off at 20 and Steve went off at 19; thank goodness I had remembered to take the mobile phone. This was quickly rectified and I soon found myself parked behind a red car with a strange man grinning at me. This time it felt different though as I only wanted him as a mate and it seemed to take the pressure off. We didn't find the decent walk or the café he knew and he didn't get anything from the charity shops but we had a nice time and I thought, 'I like this.' Steve was so easy to get on with.

I got home and later in the evening found an email from Steve saying that he had enjoyed the day but that he had wished that we could have stayed longer.

Chapter Nineteen

I sent a text to Mike telling him that I was falling in love with him and that I would wait for him unless he told me that he didn't want me. There was no reply, but I didn't feel the panic that I used to feel if I didn't hear from David. I thought of Just Maybe and his unrequited love and realised that this was a test for me. I had to just see what happened and enjoy life in the meantime. This time, being in love was not going to disable me like it had with David. I had so many things to live for and I didn't need to feel or think beyond now. I suppose all the years of disappointment and grief were at last disappearing and I could enjoy life truly again.

I remembered the day that I took Dad out in the car after he had been stuck at home for a several weeks. He looked at the colours of the leaves in the trees, and the clouds in the sky and he was amazed. Was this what seeking amazing was about?

Were Just Maybe and I in our adventure together to seek amazing going to realise that it was not just about that closeness with that special person but it was about enjoying life to the full, that that was what seeking amazing was about?

I thought of Just Maybe and wondered what he was doing and what he was feeling. Was he awake or fast asleep?

Last week I had fallen by the wayside again in my addiction to psychics and had rung two. Well, I suppose I justify it by saying that I don't spend as much on clothes as lots of other women do. When you ring a psychic you know that you are going to talk about your possible love life. Well, the second one was a bloke who claimed to be a lazy sod. He, like several before him, said that I had psychic powers so I asked what I could do with them. He was a bit stuck for an answer; during the discussion he told me that I had three men in my life and asked what their star signs were. I told him and he said that the one with the most potential was the Scorpio sign. I burst out laughing and said, 'Well, sorry mate but you've got it wrong there.' He said, 'Oh, don't you be so sure about that.' 'No, you certainly have it wrong,' I said, and he had because that was the sign of Just Maybe and there was no way that I would ever persue that route again. I do have some pride in myself, besides it was my Leo that I wanted and I would put all my psychic powers on him being the right one for me.

It was raining outside and Josh had just gone off to school. I thought of the day ahead, I really had to do some shopping; we were scraping the barrel on everything but it seemed an effort to go out in the rain. This afternoon I was going for an interview for a social work job. The agency had tried to get me to lie to potential employers to say that I wanted full-time work but I refused to do this. I had been a Social Worker for over twenty years and was good at what I did.

I could tune into the people I worked with very quickly and try to untangle their sad lives. Finding a solution which could make them happy and useful people was more difficult but I wasn't daunted by systems. I would fight for them but they had to prove to me that they were worth fighting for and they generally did. I knew that if I didn't fight nobody would. Society knew so little about these people; all they thought was that they were an embarrassment, but when it happened to them, to their family it was a different story.

I had been trying to find the key to the door which unlocked the public's knowledge and it had been a lonely cause. Many people had said to me over the years, 'Why do you bother? 'and I suppose yesterday I found the answer. Yesterday was the 3 March 2003, a magical kind of date. I had hoped to meet Mike on that day but it was not meant to be. Instead I found myself, for some strange reason, thinking about Jesus.

Yes, I am a woman of bizarre thoughts but when you are falling in love I suppose everything feels a little magical and everyone around you begins to be affected by you. I thought of the impending war with Iraq and how so many people worldwide were trying to prevent it happening and how there were people in Iraq preparing to act as human shields. I thought about what Jesus had said about love thy neighbour but the problem was that he had said to turn the other cheek, in other words be beaten by them, but that would never have destroyed their anger. So I thought about men and women and about our understanding of each other and thought that it was time for a lot more openness and honesty. What were we scared of? Making a fool of ourselves?

Jesus had said we should use love but he hadn't showed us how. Perhaps, being a cynic, he couldn't because he was a man. Now I know that any men reading this will scream but I think that female traits are more endearing to love.

At the weekend I had bought the local paper, which I do on rare occasions. My mum had read it before me and had found an article about someone we both know. I flicked through the paper after seeing what was on TV and there was a picture of Lucy. Lucy was now 14 years old. I had worked with her a year ago and here she was being sent to a detention centre.

Lucy had been one of the wildest kids I had worked with but she liked me and I liked her. She is the nearest I have ever felt to wanting to really sort someone out and although we rode several waves together when I left the job she was doing OK. But here she was being sent to the equivalent of prison and I knew how disappointed her current social worker and my ex-boss must have felt. Lucy just needed to be loved properly and I thought how lucky I was to have been given so much love in my life. Perhaps that's why I had so much to give.

Chapter Twenty

'Don't be so paranoid,' was the text from Mike. What, me paranoid? Wasn't it pretty obvious that a guy who can never get his act together to meet up when he only lives 25 miles away isn't really interested in you, that in fact he is just stringing you along. I was so mad.

Just Maybe had called me neurotic when I had asked his advice about me and Mike. He agreed that I might have blown it with him and that yet again I was going over the top. He told me not to have so much contact with Mike and to start talking about casual things like what the kids were doing and gardening. But how could I?

Yes, I was mad; that was it another set of numbers deleted from the phone and scratched out of my diary.

I sent Just Maybe an email telling him and that I was fed up with all of it and that the only thing that was good that had come out of it was having him and Steve as friends.

Yes, amazingly, halfway through our adventure and without one single phone call Just Maybe was a friend, someone I could bounce my frustrations at.

Yes, we were halfway through our adventure to experience the dating sites for six months, to seek that elusive amazing and, wow, what an adventure it was turning out to be. So what did I do after the usual floods of tears? Yes, you guessed it, I signed up for a new, different site, this time as a member rather than a visitor. 'What a fool,' you might say but like Just Maybe it is a bit like an addiction.

I thought that if Mike really had anything about him that was worth having on a permanent basis then he would have rung me but he didn't. Just Maybe said, 'Why shouldn't anyone want you?', Well, where were they then; it was always me making the effort.

I don't mind making the overtures but keeping the song going just gets so disappointing. Its just like applying for a job, doing the application form, going to the interview and then getting the call to say that you were unsuccessful on this occasion. But at least with that approach you know that there is no hope and think shall I bother again or just wait awhile.

I could live the rest of my life on my own, or pay a toy boy but that's not what I want. I want someone to come home to and get excited just before I get in the door, I want someone who challenges my views, I want so many things and it just isn't fair.

I look on the site and there are so many men there and this is the fourth site that I have been on. Oh yes, there he is with the photo that he sent to me; yes, it's Mike and he was last on the site yesterday when he said he was going to ring me, and I just think 'You shit. If you don't want me, why keep me hanging on, why make me think that none of the others mattered? I would never do that and I didn't. I tried to find someone for Brian because I didn't want to give him a false sense of hope and I thought he was a really nice bloke with a woman waiting for him. I also looked through some profiles for Steve and he followed them up.

So in my text to Just Maybe I said, 'Why can't I find someone like you? 'and hoped that he knew that I meant what I said because his friendship was so important to me that I didn't want to chase him away.

It was easy with Steve because I never fancied him but its much harder with Just Maybe because I did.But a lifelong friendship to me is more important than a regretted fling and so I steeled myself to the new search. At that moment, however, it felt like a wasted journey but I suppose when it comes down to it I am the eternal optimist, or am I?

Chapter Twenty-one

It was fun being on a new site and seeing the new talent. I found a few interesting people. I was still amazed how many plain to ugly men put their pics on and began to think that perhaps I am more attractive than I think I am.

At the moment my skin is at its best, soft and smooth. I am fortunate never to have had spots and have a colouring that some women spend fortunes to try to imitate and so when Mark said that he wouldn't even consider me without a pic, I thought, as he looked so much like the bloke out of The X–files that perhaps I should put a pic on. We had lost the lead to the digital camera months ago so Phoebe and I tried to figure out how to get a pic through the camcorder that I had bought at the Chinese New Year. I hadn't really had a go on it but Josh was like a natural film director. We gave up, it was so frustrating. So I went out to try to buy another lead but had to order one.

So I sent an email to Mark saying that I would send him a pic when I had sorted it out.

In the meantime I had had a chat with Brian and we had both agreed that it might be hard just to meet up as friends. He said that he was now looking for a casual relationship, bearing in mind how disappointing the first occasion had been I said that I didn't think once a month would be enough for me and that if I found someone else it would only complicate things and so I put Brian down to history as I thought that it was highly unlikely that either of us would ring each other. What would we have to say? So I concentrated on the new site and texted a few blokes: most replied. One of my enduring contacts has been Knightley, who I had originally addressed as his Emma. Throughout the last three months I have had emails from him and one day I went on the site to pick up some messages and he was there. So I said hello and he said that he wished that I didn't live so far away. He lived near to where David came from, about 200 miles away. I said to him that there were such things as telephones and he said he'd ring. I told him that he would have to try another night as I was going to Joshua's school to a fashion show. At the show Josh said 250 times, 'Mum, can we go…this is so embarrassing,' and it was, but I had a nice glass of red wine and I thought, 'Great,' and laughed as I thought of all the times that Josh had embarrassed me.

The job didn't materialise and I decided to look for a permanent post. I would be a lady of leisure until a job came up. I, of course, had great intentions of doing lots of gardening and becoming fitter riding my bike, and maybe I will, but my bike seems always to have a puncture and nobody mends it properly and I have two monster bushes that need hacking down, which are so tangled that even when I saw through them they just stay in a tangled mess.

Steve texted about meeting up for the day again and I said I would ring and will.

One morning I found a bloke who was a webmaster. I thought, 'Great, this is what I need, 'so I emailed him and an hour later he rang up and we had a nice chat. Then I said, 'What now?' and he said, 'I'll email you,' and this seemed very reminiscent of the Dear John email.

But one thing I have found is that I am becoming more chilled out about it all and so will wait to send Mark a pic when I can eventually sort out how to do one. there is Peter he seems as Wacky as me and is making the overtures so life is fine at the mo.

On Friday I go with the kids to meet with a Columnist from the Independent and today I oust David's junk and flog the caravan so life is fine.

Chapter Twenty-two

Being manless means that I often wake up and start thinking about things at silly times in the night, all sorts of things. I can solve all the problems of the world during those times. Being the woman I am I would probably turn over snuggle up to my man and go back to sleep. No I wouldn't; I'd probably wriggle a lot wake him up and turn him on. I am self-centred really, just like anyone else.

Recently I have been swimming most days and because of my time on the sites I look at the serious people who swim past me and rarely smile and wonder if any of them are on the sites too looking for that elusive man or woman.

I think of that energy as they swim up and down. The personal, individual energy which only benefits them; that is like being on the sites. Hopefully you learn as you go along. You learn to be more outgoing, or less over the top. But all that learning is individual learning. No one is sharing that learning.

I have only met up with Brian as a prospective partner but some men that I chat with have met several women or have met women that have met several men. Those men or women had not been right for them and some experiences have been soul destroying meetings but no one seems to think that they may suit Henry or Julie. They are just put down to experience. All that energy dispensed which could have had a happy outcome for someone else.

Yesterday I met up with Steve again. Both of us knew that it was just as friends. I don't fancy him and he has his woman. Before he came to my house I decided to look statistically at one of my sites. The one where I had met Mike and Just Maybe as really it was the one I felt most comfortable with. I didn't like the fact that you couldn't look at people six times without them knowing and thought that they might think that I was rather keen on them, when in reality I had just forgotten who they were.

I had seen a guy who I thought I had sent an email to and looked back at my prolific amount of emails and realised that the ones for November and part of December had disappeared. So I sent him another using a totally different approach and this time got favourable responses with a series of pics sent to me. He seemed a nice enough person but as I currently had myself set on The X–Files look-alike I decided to put him on a back burner.

I hadn't really done this before as I suppose I just didn't want to hurt anyone. Its just not in my nature to deliberately hurt anyone.

I had to try to untangle myself from a guy who seemed to like me a lot who was only 5ft 4in and you know that I have this quirky, somewhat old-fashioned view about the taller man.

So I looked at the statistics because I thought that, as well as writing about the emotional and practical sides of the adventure which me and Just maybe were involved in, you might also like to know the facts.

The fact is that at any time of day you will find people on the sites. And I have looked very early in the morning – 5ish, at breakfast time and right through periodically until 1am the next morning.

I don't go on so much these days as I am in more of a chill-out phase but I must spend ten minutes there nearly every day. And nearly every day there is at least one message for me. Some messages are entertaining, others are minimal and equivalent to a smile, but then they all make me feel wanted and part of this strange solitary community. The main site that I go on has no chat room and so all contacts are on a one to one basis.

So yesterday, after Phoebe had left for school at 7.30am and before I had to wake Josh at 8am, I looked at my interactions on the site since I joined on 24th November 2002.

The site allows full members unlimited messages and if you pay for a year, which is what I did, it gives you a love guarantee. They say that if you haven't found love within a year that they give you another year's membership. Whether this is true, who knows? Hopefully I won't still be there in a year's time.

Well, on 17th March I had 28 admirers. These are men who have put you as one of their favourites. The aim for many of them is that you will then make the overtures to them. My admirers were aged between 30 as the youngest and 64 as the oldest. I have never said anything to the 64 year old as I just don't want anyone that old and I think I questioned the 30 year old about his motives.

My admirers are Chamman, Cityslicker 1, Morrison 1000, Noggyn, Elpasso, Jagmanjames, 999 John, Wittygent, Zinfando, JohnWb, Gemini 6, Substitute, Urbanguy, JUST TAKE ANOTHER PEEK, Meossie, Bob No 7, Keeper of Dreams, Lonely is the Hunter, Sonofrule, Aint no soul left in these old shoes, SSGT, Peteroz, Spud56, Mossophone, Ken678, SmHall, PMY4LOVE, and Tymeglobe.

I suppose this is another reason why I am attracted to this site because I like the quirky names that people give themselves and have often made an overture email to a bloke because of the name.

By 17th March I had had 1,027 hits, that is the amount of times that my profile had been looked at. On the screen it records hits as men but it means times and so some men will have looked at my profile once whereas others have looked lots of times.

I also know of at least one other man who put me as a favourite and that was the obnoxious writer.

I currently have two favourites; I think that many moons ago I had Just Maybe as a Favourite.

You can also see how many people have looked at your profile on a particular day. On the previous day, 16th March, which was a Sunday, 21 blokes had looked at my profile of which six were my admirers.

At 7.45am on 17th March there were 44 guys and 29 girls online. The guys were aged between 21 and 56. The girls were aged between 22 and 59. There were three of my admirers who were aged 44, 45 and 46.

The site also shows people's location, which Steve thought was very helpful. Other sites just say the UK.

On 17th March of my three admirers two were from Greater Manchester and one was from Northumberland.

I sent an email to Ship to Shore, someone I hadn't seen before. His opening line said 'Hi, how are you this lovely sunny morning?' There was no reply but later in the day he had responded.

So why, with all this activity going on, doesn't the right man emerge for me?

I suppose for two reasons. Firstly, because I am too choosy. There are several men that have made positive overtures but they haven't been right for me. Secondly, perhaps because I am just attracted to the ones who don't want me.

When Steve came we went for a walk. We popped to see my mum, mainly because I knew that he would love her house, a wooden Norwegian bungalow, which she is moving from soon. Also her garden is huge, wild and backs onto the canal.

I found Steve on the ecology site and although I like him a lot he reminds me too much of my Dad; I'm not looking for a father substitute, although my dad died last July, to me he was unique and that's the way that he will stay in my memories.

I suppose I am looking for someone who is half like me and half very different to me so that there is always an element of finding out. But I know I don't want the differences to be in our moral stance I don't want another David who is a coward and deceived me through his cowardice.

Steve said that I needed someone with a strong personality who could handle me. He reckoned that he could handle me and he probably could but no, I would never go down that road as already I know that although he is turning into a good friend who gives me a welcome and farewell kiss and hug there just isn't any chemistry for me there. I am glad about that because that was the problem with me and Brian. There was chemistry and so we both knew that the friends bit couldn't work.

So Steve went home looking for houses for him and his woman and I went to the dentist. I always have problems as it kills me to open my jaw and the jabs don't work and then come into effect several hours afterwards leaving me feeling rather strange.

I have a new dentist and he is a complete dish an absolutely wonderful person to flirt with but I must admit that in his traumas of dealing with my filling it was strange to hear him call me 'babe'. I wonder how many of his other patients he calls babe. But I don't think I could live with a dentist, I'd probably dream of the drill.

Last night Phoebe wrote a letter to Tony Blair about the war but then included in it negative things about Josh. As he was tired and acting the sod anyhow, the letter went in the fire and war broke out in our house. I wondered how any new man would cope with this. You see Josh desperately needs a man in my life for his own identity and that is another reason why I have to get the right one. I won't choose someone because he will love the kids but it has to be a part of it. Phoebe and Josh got on OK with David but they have seen how he has turned out and have relatively little to do with him these days.

I am still a long way from finding my amazing but the journey doesn't seem so daunting any more. I feel flattered by the attention I have received and I haven't given up the dream so I wait patiently for the lead for the digital camera knowing that in a day or so who knows who might start looking at me in my white dressing gown.

Chapter Twenty-three

So I found myself in a new calm. It really didn't matter whether I had someone or not; well it did but not so much at least and I spent less time looking and more time just being on my own with myself.

So I put the pic on and beamed out at anyone who cared to look at me. I made my profile blatant. I didn't want a wimp any more. I only wanted men with guts who could cope with me and I got responses mostly from 30 year olds who thought, 'Here's the frustrated middle-aged woman, 'but I usually replied saying that I didn't want to be Mum. Occasionally I would think of David with his woman and then my second thought would be I'm glad its not me.

I'd get the latest on Steve's romance and he'd ask me for advice, which he would usually ignore anyhow. My contacts from Just Maybe were getting less and less so I thought he must be having a good time too.

It was as if my whole life was on the pause button, days just seemed to go by. I wasn't miserable and was really getting quite used to myself but my motivation to do anything more than the basics was low. I could see all the things I should be doing but, well, the days went by and I thought what have I really achieved today,

I read my emails and replied to them. I did kid things. I visited and spent time with my mum and thought, 'Well, I'll just have to wait, just wait until the moment is right.'

And then one night, just before I went to sleep, something happened.

I had been in the chat room and had found the computer dying on me. When I tried to go back in I just couldn't get in. I got an alert that an email had been sent to me so I read it and it was from a guy who lived four miles from me. He said that could we just meet the traditional way. I thought that I hadn't been on a date the traditional way for 30 years and so said I would sleep on it.

Just Maybe would have been proud of me restraining my usual over the top impulsive nature. And so I slept on it and the next morning said I would meet him but it took me three emails to say what I should have thought through in one.

I had also been in contact with a Teacher who felt that we could have made a go at things but my usual nature had chased him away. Anyhow, I knew that the bloke, who incidentally put himself as a high earner, had received my messages and I had given him my mobile number but I heard nothing so I sent him an email asking whether it was just a sick joke. I got no reply and then yesterday, 26th March, I had the most remarkable thing happen.

I got an email from another Mike who said that he wasn't gonna keep me hanging around, asking what was I doing on Thursday or Friday early evening. He said that he had found two pubs in my village from the Internet and could we meet.

The problem was that I couldn't remember who he was because at one point I knew about eight Mikes I didn't want to upset him by saying, 'Who the hell are you?'

So I asked him what he had been doing, in my round-about way, and he told me. I realised that he was the rock climber who I thought looked quite sweet in his climbing gear and must have told him so. Because I really couldn't remember saying anything else much to him and that must have been months ago.

So we texted and then spoke on the phone, and texted and emailed and I thought 'Blimey, I like this,' and with no hesitation agreed to meet him.

There was also a message on the phone to tell me about an interesting job that my agency had found for me and so it appeared as though the pause button had been lifted.

I had a policeman who wanted to get to know me and the bloke who had originally asked to meet came seeking a photo of me and then another remarkable thing happened.

I had emailed a guy in Orkney who was a writer and had ten published books. He had seemed rather arrogant so I thought I'd email him for a laugh really, giving the excuse that I had family in Orkney. He emailed back saying he wished I lived closer as he liked my profile and we could have had some fun together.

Of course I had to email back with one of my way over the top emails. What the hell, he was too far away and I had a date anyhow and he loved it and responded with another. I had suggested that we have a 20 year emailing affair with each other. So I sent another saying that if he had been a day earlier I would have suggested that he abandon Orkney and come and live with me. I await the response with glee.

So last night I had the latest on Steve's romance, got over a mini war with David and went to bed thinking, 'Yippee, I've got a date tomorrow with a rock climber, cum teacher, cum landscape gardener who hadn't seen my pic or my updated-for-the-12th-time profile, who just was gonna come anyhow whatever I looked like and I just thought, 'Great, this is what I've always wanted.'

Chapter Twenty-Four

Of course, sod's law happened. Mike got a call to do some supply teaching and I knew it was genuine because, after talking to me on my mobile, he also left a message on the house phone that was a bit blue, showing his natural frustration.

So the plan was that he would have a second attempt on Friday unless the school needed him for another day. He said he would ring around four to let me know what was happening. I thought he was being a bit optimistic with rush-hour traffic but was excited about this man who I knew very little about.

We had abandoned the idea of meeting at a pub. To hell with it, I thought, might as well meet him at home. He said that I could always tell him to go but I said that that was highly unlikely. Instinct told me that it was different this time. This was a real bloke with some guts, not the wimps who I seemed to have attached myself to. Sorry if I think like this but I just hate people that prat around. That's why I have so much admiration for Just Maybe. He had told me nicely that he wasn't interested. He even came back to me in a different form knowing that I might try it on again, and if I did he ignored my advances in such a nice way that, well, I just gave up in the end and realised that we were totally unsuited anyhow. I want a bloke who has the guts to tell me things whether they are good or bad. I would tell Just Maybe lots about me but I knew very little about him.

So Thursday night came and Mike and I had had a few texts and then we talked for an hour and a half on the phone. Mind you, half of it wasn't talking, it was cosmic. I have never felt like that before in my life.

Oh sure, like most brazen people who have found people over the Internet I have dabbled with cybersex but what an absolute bore, much easier to write the book and read it to someone.

This was different, a just amazingly close connection; it was really as if we were holding hands through the phone and the phone became burning hot. So I went to sleep as high as a kite and Mike said, 'You'll be fine in the morning, 'but I wasn't, I was still high as if I had had a regular two-hour supply of some illicit drug and I just had this grin fixed on my face. I was amazingly happy.

Was this what seeking amazing was really about?

Chapter Twenty-five

I had slept very little during the night and texted Mike and then spoke to him on the phone. We both hoped that he didn't get the teaching call. He was going to do some gardening for a couple of hours and then try to get to me for midday.

I was excited, but calm. I had to take our bikes to get them serviced at Halfords and decided that I would try and swim at school too. I knew I'd be pushing it but I managed to get to school for 9.35am and so was able to swim until 10am.

I had been rather a slob at home for several weeks, just doing what I had to and drifting in and out of the dating sites to see who was looking at me. So I began to panic. I decided just to shut the doors on the mess in Phoebe and Joshua's rooms and concentrate on my own just in case we ventured into it. (I was keeping an open mind.)

Over the years I have slept with the clean washing or the text books from whatever course I was doing. I don't sleep with my laptop as I'm sure I'd kick it on the floor and then have a huge and embarrassing repair bill. I could just hear them laughing when I admitted coyly that, well, actually I had gone to bed with my laptop and kicked it on the floor. I expect there would be some great jokes about what I might do to a man who shared a bed with me.

So I did the quick superficial clean-up job to the rest of the house and thought, 'I hate being such a slob.' I just couldn't justify my eccentric fun-loving nature with my slobness and then I forgot something.

This bloke was a landscape gardener and I had bags of this and that all around the back garden and some bloody impossible ugly stumps at the front of the house, which I had set fire to hoping that the house wouldn't go up in flames at the same time.

"Oh help," I thought,'What do I do? Rush madly around the garden trying to hide the evidence or jump in the bath and try to do something with my hair, which looks just like a mop?'

Oh, I so just wanted to be one of those gorgeous slim glamorous women but I knew I couldn't.

No, of course I didn't go rushing around the garden. I would just have to submit to being the pathetic woman who has a man to do the gardening. I jumped in the bath and then put all sorts of concoctions on my hair to tart it up a bit. No, I didn't look like a tart but you know what I mean.

I had decided to dress like a flower. I suppose I've never got over dressing up and I thought, by what I knew of Mike, he had a good sense of humour. So I dressed in a blue flowing skirt and a pink ripply top (one of those that fits any size of person) and I put a big yellow flower in my hair. Of course, I had the compulsory bare feet and I thought, 'Yep, I've got it right,' and I had.

This tall man walked in my front door with a huge grin all over his face and went home four hours later, still with a huge grin all over his face.

And he'd made a picnic for me too. I thought, 'Wow, surely this is amazing, just so amazingly romantic.'

Chapter Twenty-six

We had had such a fabulous time and carried on texting and talking on the phone. I knew that it would have to slow down otherwise I would have to get a mortgage to pay the phone bill. The thing was, I really didn't need to ring him because I had such dreamy thoughts and we planned to meet again soon. After having one of my silly doubts I knew that we would.

This relationship was so enabling. I could enjoy talking to my friends, watching my kids jig around with guitars pretending they were really famous popstars and find out the latest on Steve's romance. As I did this I thought of Mike and found out roughly the events of his day. It was just ace.

I got a few emails from other men and I wasn't really bothered, although the emails from the writer in Orkney were different.

He had come over as rather arrogant initially and suddenly was much more playful. He also said that he felt that he wanted to protect me. He said that I brought some sanity to his life and tried to explain what he meant but I didn't really understand him. It seemed that he had a life plan that just hadn't worked out and he liked my 'just get on with life' approach. Little did he know that I had only had that approach for such a short time. But he was right, I was much happier with that approach to life and Mike seemed to have that approach. Of course, he knew about David and the deceit and that I had zero tolerance but then he was interested in me and I in him so why should I think that he would do the same. He was very different to David, not only to look at but also his personality. I decided that whatever happened in the future I was enjoying the now and I looked forward to us meeting again. This time I would visit him and so the texts, emails and phone calls became less frequent because he was just fixed in my thoughts. I had asked if I could go and see the current garden that he was working on because a couple of weeks before I had wasted money talking to a psychic who had told me that a man was walking towards me who I would just get on with straight away; that it was my destiny and that I just had to do nothing and enjoy the experience. She had described a house with a stream in the garden and thought it was his house. I had jokingly mentioned this to Mike and he said that the garden he was currently working on had a stream in it.

Whether Mike is the man time will tell but I was certainly enjoying the experience. Life was becoming so much calmer at last.

I had asked the writer from Orkney what he wrote about as I thought that it would be fun to look at one of his books. He said that he wrote about the Internet. I had looked his name up and hadn't found anything.

One night I went in the chat room. This was before I met Mike. Online of course, I talked about the plans for meeting Mike and got the usual support, which was the reason why I still went back. They were a friendly bunch of people, anyhow I had also told them about the writer in Orkney and one of them had looked him up and found his books.

On 31st March I decided to look him up on the Amazon site and found all his books listed under the bestsellers. Then I had the most amazing revelation. I knew why I had found him and why he had responded to me. It was nothing to do with romance at all. No, I strongly believe that Mike is my romance; no, it was about who we were. He writing about the Internet and me being a social worker. You see, what I had experienced during this time of computer dating was the absolute chaos that the Internet has caused in people's lives. There are so many people who just don't know who they are any more. Look at all the men who are drifting around the sites trying to find their soulmate. And the many people outside who regard the Internet dating scene as dangerous and unnatural.

My family would cite my experiences with David as an example and Steve was caught in his feelings for a woman he had met on the net who, whether deliberately or not, lived between two men. Now this kind of lifestyle wouldn't be a problem if it was mutually agreed and people were happy but they generally weren't. I had had so many men who had said that they weren't ready to meet with me because of previous bad experiences.

Yes, the Internet in its intention, like most inventions, was good but the problem is that it was invented as a form of communication but I began to wonder where the social workers were in the invention. The people who would think of the consequences of leaving such a dangerous weapon in the hands of all and sundry. At last the authorities were trying to control the huge amount of child porn but what was being done about the other forms of chaos.

It was true that you could be anyone on the Internet. I myself had had several disguises on one of the dating sites and had changed my profile slightly but to me this had been like dressing up and just emphasising differing needs or parts of my personality. But I am strong and can cope with this.

I began to think about the man from Orkney, who appeared himself not to know what he now wanted to do. He had written about how technically to work the net but I wondered whether anyone had written about the emotional side of the net. I had entered, like Just Maybe and Mike, the most emotional part; the part where some are genuine and others not in their seek for love and what they find amazing. And suddenly I thought I must link with the man from Orkney to try to reduce these pains and dangers for adults too.

Everyone entered the dating sites on a lonely journey and no one was there to check that they were OK along the way. Perhaps that was my task and that truly amazing to me was not only finding the man or in my case men (because I now have one potential man and five new male friends) but making it safe and pleasurable for millions of people around the world.

And so instead of ringing the man from Orkney earlier rather than later, I sent him off to buy a copy of the Celestine Prophecy and said that I would ring him when he had read it because we had a task together but he had to understand first why out of all the people in the world he had met me.

Chapter Twenty-seven

I met with Mike again, this time I went to his flat. It was pouring with rain as I drove up the M6, but I didn't mind. I was so looking forward to meeting him again. We had a fabulous time together again and agreed that he would come and visit me on the following Friday.

It was April Fools day and being the wacky person I am I couldn't miss this so I went to the teddy bear factory in Telford and found a toy cat for Mike and put a special message inside the cat. I named the cat Fool Bloom, as it was April Fools day and in memory of me dressing as a flower. No, I didn't wear way-out clothes. I looked just as normal as all the other people that parked near Mike's flat.

As I left I felt the desire to stay longer and the need to see Mike again. I was just going to go with the flow. I would not plan the next 20 years in my head and I wouldn't see the demise of what felt so good. I would just enjoy this moment.

I got home, looked at the news and it was all about the latest events in the war against Iraq. I drove Phoebe to the theatre with her friend for the dress rehearsal for their annual youth theatre play. I had left my specs at Mike's house so we had talked since and shared a couple of texts. It was great meeting but didn't seem long enough.

I decided to go in the chat room but there was nobody there. Earlier in the evening I had talked to the man from Orkney and we got on very well and I thought I'd really like him as a friend.

The next evening I suddenly began to panic about me and Mike. I felt that I just didn't know what the rules of the game were. Taz (the man from Orkney) had responded to an email saying that the rules were different for each player. I suddenly remembered Tim and felt very sad. I wanted to talk to someone. David, as per usual, was on the answer phone, Mike was too, and Steve, so I rang Taz and I blurted down the phone to him saying that I had an attack of my own syndrome – 'emotional chaos' syndrome – where all these men were flooding around me and I felt in confusion. As I talked to Taz two missed calls came on the mobile; one was from Mike and the other was from Steve.

I rang Mike but he was driving and said he would be home in about 20 minutes.

I then spoke to Steve. I just felt so comfortable with Taz and Steve, a remarkable feeling of support from one person I had known just for a few days and another that I had only known for a few weeks. And then I rang Mike and I felt so at home. I knew that he was the man that both excited me and that I felt so at home with.

His accent was unfamiliar to me with its musical twang. He, like me, didn't have a voice like David had, but it suited me. He sounded so alive and caring. He listened to why I felt upset and said that he was happy about the way things were going. He couldn't see me on Friday but would come on Tuesday.

I asked if he wanted to come over the weekend but that I didn't feel that he should stay over yet. He understood and said that he would like to come sometime over the weekend. It all seemed so remarkable. A week ago he was just one of the several men that I had been in touch with and now he was beginning to be so important to me but I refused to have the pink glass this time. And as I went to sleep with Josh complaining of earache I thought how truly amazing it was to have all the men in my life, and that amazing to me, wasn't the close but insular relationship with one person. Yes, that was lovely. But amazing, to me, was not only having that but also the close friendship of others and I felt so lucky also having these other men to support me in their own different ways.

Chapter Twenty-eight

Life is so fickle. It is so strange how things can either just stay the same for so long or change dramatically in a few days.

I was out digging in the garden and a persistent robin came and hopped near me. The Robin and I had a chat together. Yes, it looked directly at me with its mouth wide open. I'm too old and long in the tooth to bother about all those daft things about signs of madness. If I want to chat to a robin, I will. So there I was digging a load of roots out that had come from the previous owners' attempt to make an easy garden, which were now leading to my frustration. The crazy thing was that the owner before them had designed an easy maintainable garden but they had put years of junk on top of it and so I was doing the excavations.

Well, Mike had said that he would come over about 11am on Sunday. At 12pm I sent a text saying, 'Where are you?' with no response. By 1pm I was getting worried that he had had an accident on the motorway and tried ringing him but he didn't answer. I had an itchy nose, which for me is like a surprise in store, and, of course, I got the surprise text at 1.20pm saying, 'Look in your porch. 'I did and there was the teddy that I had given Mike with a letter and of course the letter said that he had warned me of his self-destruct nature when it came to relationships and that he wanted to stop ours now before it went any further.

I was disappointed but not devastated as perhaps he had thought that I would be and I wondered how Brian had felt when I said the same to him. In fact I was, in lots of ways, more annoyed by the fact that he had kept me hanging around for ages.

So after half an hour of tears and the kids saying that all men are bastards, I messed around on the dating sites not really caring who was there but just as something to do as I was too clean to go out gardening and really couldn't be bothered to do much else. I also emailed all and sundry to say that I had been dumped for the first time in my life.

But, as they say, when one door closes another opens and I found a guy who looked quite cute in his pic although he was smaller than I usually go for. We exchanged a few emails and he asked for some pics, not only of me but of the kids as well. I said that I would email them to a private address; he gave me his email address but pointed out that I would know his surname.

He had said that he was in the music business when I had asked him what he did and I had joked about that saying it must be good for pulling women. He was also looking for a wife. I had never responded to ones for wives before but thought, what the hell. I couldn't really care. So I sent the pics and I got a reply saying he didn't want to be blunt but that basically he didn't fancy me.

It was disappointing. He turned out to own two night clubs with R & B bands so it would have been quite fun and a totally different world to mine but then it wasn't meant to be.

So I carried on digging and chatting to my robins because, in fact, there were two of them.

I had texted Mike to tell him not to worry and he had texted back to say that he was sorry that he was such a coward and that he hadn't talked to me directly.

And the next day I went off to Wales on my own to my caravan, which is based on one of the old Butlins sites.

It was Tim's birthday and although he had been dead for two years I had the urge to spend the day, in spirit at least, with him alone. Also, I needed to go and see if the winter had caused any damage to the caravan.

It was a beautiful day as I drove and for most of the day I felt very happy. This time on my own was paying off. I was really beginning, for the first time in my whole life, to enjoy my own company. I realised what a nice interesting person I was to be with.

In his letter Mike had described me as lovely and exciting, which I think I am. So instead of talking to the robin in the back garden, I started talking to Tim and I played songs that he liked from time to time and some of them really loud, which he liked but I never used to when he was alive and I was living with him.

Yes, most of it was nice but, of course, there were times when the tears flooded down my cheeks as particular pieces of music brought back particular memories or looks on Tim's face.

And on the journey home I had to change the tunes as I didn't want to arrive home and get questions from family members about why I had been crying. I chose not to remind them that it was Tim's birthday. I had had a nice day and I had told Tim that it was up to him to find me a man and that he needed to stop bewitching me.

I checked my email and had a lot of replies. As a response to being dumped I had changed my name to 'Wacky, Impatient but lovely' and said under the description about yourself that I was pissed off, followed by the original blurb. The response had been incredible; in one day I had had 36 men look at my profile compared to the usual half a dozen and in three days I had had about 250 hits and I had removed the pic. So I had hit gold with the name and the profile but I didn't really care it was just something to do.

I had been trying to get David about our website and so the following morning decided to see if he had at last got it up and running. Before I looked, of course, I had to check the emails and there were a couple of interesting ones including a new bloke who came from Mike's site who I had never come across before and was fairly local; he said he had a legal background. He turned out to be a prison officer who was on a week's leave, with two grown-up children. He had put in his profile that he was 44 but admitted straight away that he was 48 so I told him that he was daft lying and that I really didn't see the point.

Another guy said that he had also been dumped this week but that he was glad because the woman he had met had said that she was 46 but he reckoned that she was more like 56. He said that he wasn't ageist, he just didn't like the fact that she had lied about her age.

I had found myself becoming more and more direct. I only wanted a bloke who could deal with me and have me as I am. I was becoming less over the top; I suppose the novelty had worn off but I also no longer did the intro flirting. I just didn't see the point. In fact I was really at the stage of not bothering at all.

I knew that David would just laugh if I said that I wouldn't bother but to me looking on the sites was just getting like playing the computer at a game of cards. It was something to do just because there was nothing better to do.

I began to believe that what one psychic had told me recently, that I would not find my man through dating sites, was in fact becoming true.

I decided to write one of my books but had a problem; Windows wouldn't open and so I decided just to leave the laptop online and see if any emails appeared during the day.

I was not going to waste the good weather looking at a list of men's names and thinking who the hell is he, looking at the profile and then realising, oh yes, its him, the one with four kids and a smoker. I didn't like the fact that he would now know that I had looked at him again and think I must be interested.

Anyone reading this will believe that this is a fantasy but I assure you that it is all true. I was just going off down the stairs when I had the familiar noise that announced the arrival of an email; I thought it might be from the Prison Officer but it wasn't, it was from Mr Drool himself, a guy I had really fancied from about a month ago who I had done my usual over the top stuff with. We had talked about me waiting in his queue. He had said that he had two queues a long one where the women had no pics and a short one with pics. It was at the time when I had problems with the digital camera and so by the time I had sent him the required pic, he had received it and said that he had already agreed to meet someone and wasn't a serial dater and wanted to see how it went.

Whenever I went into that site I had to have a look at him; he just looked so welcoming, slouched on his settee, and my wonderful imagination could place myself in his arms. I really didn't know much about him but my level of fancying equalled the way I used to feel many moons ago about Just Maybe. On this site he didn't know when I was looking at him either.

So I thought, just as I forgot who Mike was, he had forgotten who I was. But to ask for another pic showing the whole of me must surely be the cruellest blow that anyone can give but I had to send him one didn't I?

Chapter Twenty-nine

I decided to go back to the site where you could whisper to each other. I had got bored with doing this but thought, well, a few weeks had gone by and perhaps a few more interesting men might emerge.

Steve was spending a week entertaining his daughter and I planned to go to the caravan. Now that Mike wasn't in my life I suppose I just fell into my old ways except for shorter periods of the day. So I did start to do some gardening and some of the other tasks, which had seemed so dull in comparison to seeking out new men from the cattle markets, which were disguised as dating sites; that was the way that I was feeling about them.

I had a family pic on one of the sites the one with the whispers, and a few men approached me for whispers. I looked a few up from the picture gallery that they had on site. Its incredible how long two minutes seems when you are waiting for a reply. This site timed all of your whispers.

So I found a couple of interesting people and gave them my email and had a couple of men from another site to email. It filled the time and then I decided to email Mike 44.

I missed him and wondered whether he missed me too. He replied and I phoned him and we had a nice chat but at the end of it I missed him more and sent him an email asking if I could have a second chance.

Back on one of the sites I found a man who was an inventor. One morning, after I had seen Phoebe off to catch her bus and was killing some time before I woke Josh up, I chatted to my inventor and another man who both seemed quite nice but both lived rather a long way away from me. Suddenly I got the sound which alerted me to a whisper and so I looked at the profile of the man who had sent it and he was married.

Well, there was no way that I would contemplate someone who was openly married even though he said he was looking for friends. I've heard that one before but I thought I'd reply just for the hell of it and after the second whisper I asked him where his wife was and he said that she was busy; she was a politician and he had to accompany her to Paris next week. He said that he liked me which I thought was a bit over the top for a couple of whispers and he asked if I would be on the site later. I asked him what time because, of course, by now I was intrigued to see whether what he said was true or why he would make up such a story. Fortunately I hadn't got any great plans for the day and so I decided that I would try to go on the site about ten minutes after he said to try and quiz him.

I had decided to go swimming and as Phoebe was finishing school for Easter at lunchtime I had to fit it in quickly. But just as I planned to go I got a call about a job that I had been interested in doing. They had originally wanted a full-timer but it turned out that the person that they were going to use lived too far away and so they had thought of me. And so I had to make a call to the manager. This meant that I was later back from my swim than I had planned and so was later going online. There was no sign of my politician's husband and I had stupidly failed to write down his identity but instead I chatted to a man who lived half of his time in Oslo and half of his time in the UK. We got on very well and were able to chat freely to each other about things but, even so, chatting with a minute delay all the time is such a strange way of communicating.

I suppose the thing that I value most is good communication and that is why at times I get so cross with David when he deliberately ignores me. I like people to be reliable and he just isn't.

As I have gone through this experience over the last few months I have realised how just for our own needs, we delude ourselves. We chat to people who seem so warm and friendly but they fail to understand our needs. Often men talk about being honest and sincere but whether their interpretation of the words are mine or other women's, I question. Men also talk about being baggage-free, which basically means not having previous women in their lives or kids. Yesterday the man from Oslo said that his kids were off his hands because they were 21 and 24 implying that Phoebe and Josh would hamper any relationship that we would have. But none of us are baggage free because of history and of things that remind us of events in our lives and how we responded to them.

I suppose another aspect which I haven't openly explored is the balance between excitement and fear.

Just Maybe had read about my feelings for Tim and the love I had felt and had said it must be exciting to contemplate the different love of another man; I suppose it is but it is also frightening. I think about the men that this could have happened with and, of course, the first was Just Maybe but he said that it was all too fast and he panicked.

This has been a theme for me throughout the time on the Internet; I suppose that I have made it fast because I just wanted to know how much any of these men could really cope with. The truth is that so far, in terms of love and individual companionship, I haven't found anyone that can cope with this.

Just Maybe would advise me to slow down. He has waited a few days before replying to emails from women that he fancied but I just can't do that. I'd rather take the risk because in the long run it just wouldn't work for me.

I have also said that it is a shame that we can't help each other more, that we can't help the newcomers and support the long-enduring. I find that people who have just joined one of the sites want to know how many men you have met up with and how it has gone. I suppose that my track record of two for romance and two as friends out of, I imagine, at least 100 men is really not very good. The long-endurers seem to hang in there just hoping that the next one will be the ONE.

But in our personalities we have strategies to attract and mechanisms to defend, kinds of push/pull factors to test out the new people that we come across. There is a strong fear of failure.

I have also come across lots of men who assume that a relationship just has to be the full works man/woman thing and are surprised when I tell them about my relationships with Steve and Just Maybe. I suppose when I think about them sometimes I am amazed too.

I have reached the stage now, on 11th April, where I am sifting. The guy I talked to yesterday talked about sex in terms of quality rather than quantity when I told him that up until going on the sites I had only had sex with two men, and I agreed. It is the same with the list of men who I email there are some who I have emailed to say I assume you don't want to be in touch any more and they email back to say, 'Of course they do, 'and then I never hear from them again and delete, them from the address book. They are the equivalent to the admirers. On one site now have 38 but what are they admiring? Nothing really, just two minutes of amusement at my latest name. Its impressive to say that you have 38 admirers but what means a lot more are the now very obvious two really good friends, Steve and Just Maybe.

Oh and I know that most women reading this might still think that Just Maybe and I would get together at the end of my journey but the chances are very small because he has his woman and because, although he really is becoming that close friend that you dream of having, he has such awful stubborn streaks and is so selective in what he will attend to and what he will ignore. I will send him an email and he will respond to half of it and ignore other bits and the bits he always ignores are the deep emotional bits. Steve, on the other hand, will explore these deep emotional bits. But then you see I never fancied Steve and Steve said that he never fancied me.

Last night Just Maybe sent me a small piece that he had written about the events in Iraq with the tumbling of Saddam's statue but he sent no explanation with it and I wondered what he was saying to me. There was no, 'What do you think? It was in a follow-up email that an explanation came.

I had previously suggested that perhaps we should ring each other. We had a pact, at the beginning of writing all of this, that we wouldn't phone until the book was finished, but last night was an example of how a phone call would have sorted out things better.

In contrast, at 12.10am, when I was in the chat room, a text came from Steve saying to have a good holiday as he knew I was going to the caravan. In fact, I was now going later than originally planned. I immediately rang him and said that I was in the chat room and he came in. For the next 20 minutes we used the chat room and then, when I crashed I rang Steve on the mobile. The communication I have with Steve is wonderful; we just freely contact each other when we feel like it, knowing that if the other is busy when they are free they will respond.

Last night Just Maybe said he wanted my opinion because I knew him. I do but not as well as he knows me because he will only share selective parts of his personality with me. I wonder whether this is just the way he is or whether he feels the things he doesn't share are exclusive to his girl/ boyfriend relationship. He loves giving me advice and being fatherly or brotherly, whichever one it is to me. I also wonder how much of it is Just Maybe and how much is his northern cultural roots.

Very early on in the book I had thought about the few black men that I had come across on the sites. In fact, I have not chatted with any black men in the time that I have been online. Just Maybe said that he had seen several black women but whether he has chatted with them I don't know. I have also only seen one physically disabled man online.

Chapter Thirty

'I am confused, why are you so active on the site if you don't want to go out with anybody?' was the email I received from Peter.

I had previously noted an email from another guy entitled Wow, with a really nice message saying that he had two ponies, which he thought the kids would like, and was building a tree house.

The trouble was I had forgotten who the first one was and nearly missed even seeing the second one.

So I sent a sorry to the first and then realised that he was the prison officer that I had nearly gone out with but chickened out.

The second was much more interesting but he was 52 and was really at the upperlimit of the age group that I wanted to date but I sent him a reply and then I looked at his profile and saw the most wonderful romantic blurb at the end, which I wondered whether he wrote or got from a book. So I sent another email saying that if he gave me a champagne picnic (cos he was a high earner), then I would buy a posh frock and be happy to get it dirty. This was going to be in his tree house, of course.

I had come across two men, one who said his first date would be in Paris and the second who wanted his first date in Barbados. I asked them both who would pay and both said that they would. I giggled with Phoebe about this; it was like a non-televised version of blind date. We both thought that it would certainly be a make or break situation.

I was getting on with the garden a bit better and was having fun rediscovering the old garden underneath the years of neglect. I would have liked to have rung Mike to tell him but I thought I better not. I had noticed that he hadn't been on the site for a week.

Every time that I went on the Internet there were emails waiting for me.

While I was in the garden I chatted away to my robin and then suddenly there were not only two but three robins in the garden. I thought that this was like the dating sites where more than one bloke seemed to come along at the same time.

On one of the sites there was a man advertising himself openly for sex. Of course, I had to ask him how much; then, bugger it, the computer crashed and when I got back he had gone. So computer dating is daunting and extremely frustrating but it can also be fun.

I suppose that my whole idea of amazing has developed over time away from that one and only relationship to something much greater, the ability to find all sorts of interesting people all living in the UK. I have chatted to all sorts of people and today came across a musician who could also compose music. I hope that he keeps in touch.

I feel however that I am coming to an end of phase one in the Internet dating scene and am about to enter phase two. In phase one I was hunting; in phase two I will wait to be hunted and if nobody wants to chase me then I shall just carry on talking to the robins in the garden.

Chapter Thirty-one

And so I entered my passive phase. This didn't mean that I never went online. I had to do that, but I sort of hung around like everyone else did and on Just Maybe's site I sent people winks and kisses instead of words. Oh, and of course, I changed my name and profile again and sent a pic that was waiting in the queue to go online.

I became 'Better than a back of a bus' and wrote a story, which included a prince coming to look for me, and sent a photo with me, the kids, the rabbits and the hamsters all grinning together. I thought, well, I only want the man who wants all of us and so if he doesn't like Shaggy our black hamster I might have problems anyhow. The pic went in the queue but the profile was there after a day and 23 men looked at it in the first day. I wondered what it would be like to have no one look at you.

One guy who had sent regular emails and was good looking got into a bit of dialogue and so I sent him an email saying that when I got to 2,000 hits, would he meet me. I am currently on 1,750 but don't yet know his reply. And so after ten mins I went across to another site and found three men who I had exchanged whispers with and all three started chatting to me but only one of them really had something to say.

I had seen him on that site a couple of months before but didn't remember much about him. He didn't remember me because I had a different ID but when he told me that he was at college doing IT I remembered who he was. We got chatting and I told him about my frustration with my website, which David was supposed to get up and running but was dragging his feet over. He said that he did web design and so I asked if I could pay him to get it going. He said that he would be interested but that I needed to know that he only had partial vision. There was this good-looking guy replying just as quickly to me as anyone else with only 40 per cent of his vision. I said that I would ring him when I came back from my holiday at the caravan.

All sorts of things went through my mind. I wanted him to do it maybe partly because I thought it would be good for the image of the site. But also for my sense of justice, why shouldn't he do it; I would ring him.

I thought of what it would be like to date someone who is partially sighted. I would always have to drive unless we had taxis. I also wondered what it would be like to know that he couldn't see me properly. It sent all kinds of feelings through my system.

So off out into the garden I went to put all the prickly hedge on the top of the skip. It is at these times that I feel jealous of women who have the man to do these things, but then a lot of men would leave it for the woman to do anyhow.

It was the first real day of the Easter holidays and I was enjoying having the kids hanging around. Josh had a friend round to play and we all went off swimming and then on to McDonald's. We played the family game on this child as it was the first time we had had him in the car and it has become a bit of an initiation game. We get to a clear bit of road and I drive at top speed open the windows and play an appropriate piece of music full blast. On this occasion it was a mix of 'Grease', which seems always to be around and goes well with the occasion. The child in question loved it like all kids do and so I got my 'cool' mum status.

He wanted to stay over so we went round to his house to ask his mum and found her breast feeding a baby with her husband, his step-dad creeping around quietly. I thought about how different it was to the way my two were brought up; I would crash bang around them so that they now sleep through anything. I could get the vac out and tidy their bedrooms and they still wouldn't wake up.

I suppose this is one of the reasons I have been reserved in this dating game because, having had some of David's habits to deal with, I wonder what the next bloke's will be. But then, if we really love each other, I imagine we will just sort it and come out shouting, crying and laughing – hopefully mostly laughing.

For some reason I decided to listen to my voicemail on my mobile. Its supposed to tell you if you have a message but mine rarely does. Not many people ring the mobile anyhow but today there were two messages and both from Natural Friends; the second caller had said that he would ring back after six and at two minutes past six there was a message. He sounded dishy so I thought I'd ring him first. He turned out to be a dairy farmer with three kids in Wiltshire. One of his sons answered the phone. We had a nice long chat with interruptions from both lots of children. I told him that he sounded nicely eccentric; he was pleased by this and remarked that he had never thought of himself like that but that he probably was because he didn't fit in with the local farmers' scene. It seemed as though, since separating from his wife four years ago, he had had several girlfriends but that he was looking for his soulmate. We had a discussion about what people actually meant by their soulmate. He felt that it was someone you wanted to be with all of the time whereas I believe that is someone who is always there with you in spirit but doesn't have to be there physically. It was an entertaining discussion but I couldn't see myself as a farmer's wife. I said I would keep in touch and I probably will.

And then I had an email from Knightly; he had picked up my

new name and I sent an email back saying I had lost his phone number. He sent an email back about him being in a pile of sweaty bodies. He always makes me laugh.

Chapter Thirty-two

So off we went to the caravan. Josh said he wasn't going to go because I wasn't taking the laptop with me. I told him that there were going to be too many kids around with Annette's lot there and besides he was becoming a computer bore. I hadn't bought a caravan in Wales for him to ignore the world outside.

When we got there the weather was beautiful just like a nice summer's day. Shorts and T-shirts weather. We were going to have nearly a week on our own before Annette, my sister in law, arrived with her kids. My pair moaned and swore like the troopers they are and so I thought, 'What the hell am I doing here?' It was a mixed bag of good and bad; I had over a week without any emails or staring at the whisper screen whilst popping to do jobs around the house between messages.

I had said that I would go into passive mode and I did; well, I wasn't totally passive, I was responsive. I had contact with four men whilst I was there: a chat with the guy with two horses who turned out to have six; a sonnet and couple of texts from a man from Buxton; and chats and texts from Steve and Knightly.

One day I had about 15 texts from Knightly and I sent him a soppy one saying that if in two year's time, he had no one, he should ask me to marry him and I'd probably say yes. He asked why I needed two years to play the field. I said just because I never had and wanted to know what it was like.

I had had the two short flings; now it was time to get to know several men at the same time purely as friends and see what got chucked up in the wind. It was time for me to chill out.

So Annette came and I realised how lucky I was only having two children instead of four and all boys too. I had pleaded with Phoebe and Josh to cut out the swearing and go into delightful children mode and they did.

Annette couldn't understand me messing with all this dating stuff but then she has someone she can speak to several times a day even if he is away, which I don't.

So we had the barbecue because after the sunny days and rainy days there were sunny ones again and, of course, I did what I always say I won't ever do again – drink beer and wine in the same session.

It was funny getting Annette to chat with Steve and Knightly on the mobile with me giggling in the background. The thing was that I reckon they both fancied her too but then they are my mates so I wasn't that bothered.

I even got to talk to David to tell him we were having barbecued bacon, which he had introduced me too. Then, in the middle of the night, I spewed up, had a panic attack and felt like the loneliest soul on earth. Oh, and I missed Tim so much.

So I decided to go home a day early. The weather was pretty horrible again anyhow and so we saw Annette and her kids off on a trip on the Ffestinniog Railway and we headed for the nearest little chef only to find that they had no pate, my pancake wasn't that brilliant and Josh, for the millionth time, wanted a pudding and wasted three quarters of it. In the past I would have eaten it myself but now I just growl at him.

So we drove home and even in the rain Wales looked beautiful and I thought that the weather had been just like me, happy and sad muddled up together.

I am fortunate that I am never down for long but I told Steve and Knightly how I felt and they were fantastic, just there for me, watching over me, just the way that you want true friends. and so Seeking amazing is so much part of it for me; these men, who were complete strangers a few months ago could now be contacted anytime to share just anything. They made me reassess the situation.

Josh asked what time we would get home so that he could continue building his castle and army on the computer and see how 22, one of the rabbits, was because Granny had reported that she wasn't eating. Thank goodness she was OK. We lost Shaggy, one of the hamsters, once; he went under the floor boards in my bedroom. I felt so sad and thought, I'm not buying a replacement.' Then, at about 2am the next morning, David went to make himself a cup of coffee after a marathon computer session – probably emailing the other woman – and there was Shaggy running around the kitchen. How he had found his way there, goodness knows.

So we arrived back home and no, I didn't go straight on the computer. I spent time sorting out the kids and making my bed, which I should have done before I left but I do hate changing double duvet covers.

About 9pm I looked at my emails; there were 27 and 3 in the bulk and most were from some bloke or other. I thought that it was a nice welcome home.

Just Maybe had sent me an Easter card and a note saying that he didn't like an idea that I had for the book; I thought I couldn't be bothered to answer. Usually I wrote back straight away but this time I didn't bother. I was more interested in the other emails. I went on the whisper site and the man from Oslo said, 'Hello sexy,' which I thought was a nice boost. I didn't really feel that sexy but he had a pic so it was encouraging. We had quite a nice chat and I said that he should come and see me and he said that he might but I thought, of course, he won't.

On another site a guy about an hour away from me seemed keen to get to know me. I decided to reassess the possible men who I might be interested in and who showed an interest in me and was surprised to find that there were eight. I told Steve and he seemed pleased for me. Knightly was still taking a keen interest in me; perhaps he was amused by my distant suggestion.

I had a long phone call with the composer and we found lots of common interests but as he lives in East Anglia I think that he is a long shot.

The man with the six horses sent a short email to say that he was working the next day but that he would ring me in the evening.

So I had two late nights chatting to men and then on the Saturday after chatting to Steve and Knightly I had a long chat with the new guy Dave. He said that he had chatted to a lot of women and had suggested meeting up but they backed down; he was getting rather fed up with it all. I said I would meet with him and I will because I now think that it is best to meet several men on a friendship basis. To add to this, he is a chiropodist and it was only a few days ago that I said to Phoebe that I must do something about my toenails but I think a first date talking about and tampering with feet is rather a bit too much.

I sent a text to the man from Oslo saying that I wanted him to send me an email address as I didn't want to go on the site much more as it was too time consuming but that I wanted to keep in touch with him. I hope he sends it because out of the current eight he is one of the two that I like the best but, as I'm chilling out, if he does that's great and if he doesn't then it just wasn't meant to be; but then a trip to Oslo does sound a nice idea

Chapter Thirty-three

Saturday, 26th April 2003 was one of the most time-consuming days. I just did nothing but talk to men, not on the Internet but on the phone. It was lovely but when it got to 9.30pm and the kids still hadn't had their tea, well, I thought, you evil woman. Mind you, they did have their dinner at 3pm so it wasn't that awful and it was a Saturday. But I just can't turn possibilities away and that's what they all were, stronger than usual possibilities and all wanting to know me.

Suddenly that spell that I had concocted, ha ha, had worked and I had eight men who were interested in me and Steve and Knightly still checking that I was OK.

I was back from holiday and hadn't responded to Just Maybe's emails. I suppose I just found them low priority. I wasn't particularly bothered about him rejecting my ideas; it's just that he seemed so distant now our friendship was the same as it was three months ago. Having had the wonderful banter with Steve and Knightly I just couldn't be bothered any more. I think that was the way I felt about lots of the men that I had made contact with over the last few months. I knew that I would never contact Mike 44 again. What was the point? It was all just one-way traffic. No that's not quite true. Just Maybe had sent me an Easter card but I found that I didn't wait for the 20 emails saying not a lot any more; I just got on the phone and talked to the men. They could suss me out and I could do the same. I suppose that I was just more confident and knew that I was really the exciting, lovely person that Mike had said I was in his letter when he dumped me. I had liked Mike and I had wished that I hadn't gone over the top. I think that he would have been a good friend. I talked to Knightly about it and he said that just because you have sex with someone doesn't mean that you couldn't be friends with them afterwards but I suppose that Mike just thought that I would dominate him like Just Maybe did. But strangely enough it was Just Maybe who dominated me. He was the one who wanted the book to stay just as it was. He didn't think that readers wanted to know how it was written. He wanted to keep the adventure and I suppose I agreed with him but would anyone really believe that all of these things and these feelings were actually true?

One of my new men, Victor, had shown an interest in the book. He was an interesting character because he only worked when he needed to and had what he described as a chequered life. He was currently filling his days writing, taking dogs for walks and supporting his daughter. He said that in the past he had made a lot of money but also spent a lot of money. I found him intriguing and wanted to meet him just to find out more.

I suppose in my adventure this is where I had got, not in the heavy romance state but the intriguing state. Victor was interesting and so were the other seven men. Of course, there is always one that you dream will be the one and, of course, it was the man from Oslo; there was just something about him. But then I was now living with my eyes wide open and realised that the chances of ending the journey with him were as likely as Just Maybe or Richard Gere.

Even the most charming of size 16 women with competitive page-three boobs who is ordinary-looking gets passed over for possibilities of better-looking women who may never emerge. Men are nice to you when they say they have changed their mind when they see your pic but I often think, 'Well, you say you are good looking but you are not. I suppose I shouldn't share these bitchy thoughts but then someone has to, don't they?

I had an email from a guy who had a whole website selling himself, talking about online dating and showing his own personal horoscope but his email to me was so neutral it was beyond belief. How was I supposed to know whether he was interested in me or not? So different to Dave who wrote lovely bubbly replies and said, 'Tell me more. I liked him but he was smaller than I go for and I wondered how many emails it would take to get the vital phone call. Until then I would continue to be amused by Knightly, chummy with Steve and intrigued by Victor.

My chiropodist had backed down on meeting up; he said that our chat on the phone had made things from the past resurface but perhaps that was just another way of saying, 'I don't like your pic much, Rache. 'Only time will tell.

It had been raining a lot and Josh and I had giggled as we stood under a great big umbrella at the garden centre. We were buying fruit bushes and vegetable seeds and I wondered whether my robins were waiting for me in the garden. I hadn't seen them since I had been back from my holiday. I was feeling rather disgruntled as Phoebe had lost the car keys, which had keys for everything on them, the washing machine was broken and several other things in the house needed attending to and I thought, 'Is this a sign should I just submit to spending my life with Knightly, who would sort it all for me?' But as I thought this I listened to the birds singing, watched the horse munching in the field next to our garden and thought how two people had told me how nice Oslo was.

Chapter Thirty-Four

Phoebe had lost the car keys which contain the keys for our house, Mum's house, our old house key, which Mum is buying off me and used to also have the caravan key but, fortunately, I had left that with Annette. It was so frustrating; we had looked everywhere and both me and Phoebe had got cross about it. The washing machine wasn't working and I was using the one that I had left at the old house and I couldn't get in to use it. Anyhow at five o'clock I found them tucked behind the wok. She must have chucked them down in her temper. I thought that she had had an argument with Josh but it was all about not finding a particular video.

So the day got in a muddle and after the previous day where I spent all that time talking to blokes I really felt like an inadequate housewife. But Josh and I went to the garden centre with the spare set of car keys and the fruit bushes got planted.

For the first time in ages I watched some tele and I really enjoyed it. I didn't go on the net until about 10.30pm and there were no emails for me. Actually I had popped on just before the first programme started at seven and found two new men offering to get to know me from two different sites so I sent them my email address.

And then I went on to the whisper site later and Victor and the man from Oslo were there. I didn't go over the top. I suppose I didn't really mind if I did with Victor as he is a bit over the top himself but this time I really wanted a good chance with the man from Oslo. Interestingly, he wasn't as slim as the usual men I go for but he had called me Sexy and it just felt nice.

He said that he had had Swedish friends staying all weekend and that he would email me tomorrow. I told him to email when he was ready because he knew that I liked him and that this time I wasn't going to go over the top and I am trying hard not to. He had been able to stand his own in our discussion but had also listened to my viewpoint, he had talked sense, not just seedy flirty talk, and I just hoped that he would want to stay in touch. I had to make sure that I didn't either try to push him away or offer too much of myself too soon.

Steve had been to see his daughter and so I texted him to see if he was home. He had just got back and so I rang him and then we both went online and found someone in the chat room. This was a strange experience talking to Steve and being online at the same time in a strange tripartite discussion but with two out of the three of us being more in the know.

I commented to Steve about having a discussion with Knightly, how Mike 44 had called me Mrs No Knickers and the origins of the name. He, like Mike, had found it a complete turn on. Steve just laughed and it seemed to do nothing for him and so I said this proved that just being friends was right for us. The day before one of the men I talked to who initially wanted to meet up but later in the day, after seeing my pic, changed his mind didn't believe that men and women could just be friends. But Steve and I are and I am with Knightly, although I imagine if I lived nearer to him he'd probably like to be more.

I went to bed pleased that I hadn't chased the man from Oslo away but still thinking that I would be surprised if I got an email from him.

I had a restless night, it was a back to school night for Phoebe and normally she would just go to sleep but she kept calling for me saying that she couldn't go to sleep and that she was worried that she wouldn't wake up. And then Josh was roaming around; he wasn't going until Tuesday and he eventually got into bed with me and we had an old wriggle bum and snatch-the-duvet night.

I woke early; the birds were singing away in the garden and I began to reflect on the last four to six months and thought what an exciting adventure I had had in the world of online dating. What a lot I had learned, not only about it, but also about myself. The day before had been frustrating but when I had found the keys and gone to collect the washing I had chatted with my old next door neighbour, who was a social worker too. I realised that I had never told her about me and David splitting up. She reminded me of an occasion soon after we had got together when one day he just wandered off and I hadn't known where he had gone. I had worried about him because he had rung up in a distressed state.

I told her all about the online dating which she was amused by and said that it sounded as though I was having a great time. I suppose in lots of ways I am but when I think how lonely I was the other day I would still so like to have just that one man who I can come home to and get excited about, but this time someone who wants to spend significant time with me. At the moment I really don't know who the hell he is.

Meeting all these men and documenting the experience has been wonderful and hopefully will be helpful to other people in the future but dealing with a lot of the feelings has been hard. It is hard to know that you are judged just by the way you look or the few words that you write and that there is such a strong selection process. All the traits of too tall, too short, too fat, too thin.

Even the idea of your ideal person is just so strange.
When I first knew Tim I thought that he was quite ugly. But then there was just something about him and one day I sat on the floor

leaning up against the chair that he was sitting in. There were a crowd of us teenagers and not enough seats. We were all mates and at the time I was going out with someone else so we just sat anywhere. I sat there and Tim tickled me for fun on the neck and that was it, the chemical magic that led very soon after, to me splitting up with my boyfriend and spending the next 28 years with him as the most significant person in my life.

And as I write this he has been there with me in my thoughts and at times it's as if he has been writing the book with me. The events of my story and the men who have emerged are just so amazing that no one would believe that they are all true.

One day I talked to the man from Orkney about the fact that I got twos of everything and that I had eight Mikes. I had joked that it was Tim bringing them all to me using binary and as a computer man who started with them in their infancy he understood the significance of binary. The man from Orkney pointed out that eight was a computer number too.

Yesterday and today are the 27th and 28th of the month and in five months' time it will be Phoebe's and my birthdays. I wonder where I will be by then? Three years ago from then Tim came to visit us and it was then that I realised that he really wasn't part of my life any more.

When I met David I didn't know what he looked like and didn't fancy him but I was so in love with him. The style of the chat room seemed so different to the online dating as, like when I first knew Tim, you were part of a crowd and just gradually beamed in on a few people. Online dating is like choosing the right product from a shop. You have a selection of products with certain specifications, that are supposed to do certain things. You then test them out but the products are two-way, they answer you back and, depending on how they answer you back, or you answer them lead either to excitement or disappointment.

It is exciting getting emails nearly every time I go online but then the times there aren't any is disappointing. But if, like me you go online three times a day, what do you expect? People have their own lives doing those ordinary things but it would be nice to have a machine which could probe people's minds to know whether they were thinking about you or whether they just thought you were a joke. A lot of time and heartache would be saved, but then we are human beings and maybe that's why, for a lot of us, this method of dating is so hard because it is so inhuman and so potentially clinical.

I have thought and said on many occasions that there should be much more guidance. Not only about the potential dangers about meeting a stranger but also about the emotional side. Many people are vulnerable and getting someone interested in you can throw up all sorts of things from your past.

Just Maybe had picked a woman with the name Storyteller and had remembered a different significance of the name. One day I was looking at pics and saw a man who I thought looked quite nice and Phoebe came to have a look. She said, 'Mum you can't go out with him, he looks just like Dad,' and I looked again and I suppose I could see what she saw.

I always want to know from the start what went wrong before and I suppose this causes a great deal of heartache for men who are trying to bury their past. David sticks his head in the sand. He is very good at dealing with other people's problems but not his own.

This approach chases a lot of men away but I know that my man will be someone who can face anything with me. That doesn't mean that we agree on things but that we can work through things and learn to compromise in a way that doesn't demean the other. I want a true friend but I also want a lover and someone who has their own identity but who relishes mine.

Chapter Thirty-five

I was waiting for a call from my solicitor and so had the mobile on the ringing tone rather than silent. A text arrived from Knightly. I replied and then another came. I loved getting texts from Knightly; they generally either made me laugh or were warm and supportive. But today I didn't want the phone bleeping as I had only been in this job for three days so I sent a reply saying not to text and that I would be in touch later.

After sorting out Phoebe with a lost swimming costume and bunging some nuggets for a quick tea for Josh in the oven, I rang Knightly and we chatted for about ten minutes and then he was off to have his tea. I took Josh to the theatre and popped around to David's to give him the voting card. He looked rather tired and said that he had had a busy day.

I asked when I was going to meet the other woman and then said that it just didn't matter any more, and it didn't. Me and David were well and truly history. He was now a friend that I would see from time to time and that felt right.

I messed in the chat room for a bit after eating a Chinese take-away with Phoebe.

I then went to pick up Josh and after the children went to bed a text arrived from Knightly so I replied. Then he sent another and after about the fourth text I rang him and said that he was in a strange mood and we just talked and talked. He said that he thought that he had never been in love and I talked about being in love with David and with Tim.

He had sent me an email which had made me laugh and I had sent it to David, Just Maybe and Steve. And as we talked and I found out more about Knightly, I suddenly realised that I was like Emma. I had blindly missed what was right in front of my eyes, that Knightly was my man, that up until now I had deluded myself and I told him so. We planned that he should come to stay with me in the spare room, as friends, the following weekend. We said, 'Let's go with the flow, 'but you know me, can I?

I think my journey has come to an end and I've found amazing. That man who is just so giving, so warm, so funny and who will happily come and repair my broken shower. That man who is just so interesting and yet, like Emma, I just didn't see it before and the fact is that he likes me so much. Now isn't that just truly amazing?

Chapter Thirty-six

Word broke and whatever I tried to do I just couldn't get into it. I was so frustrated because I thought that this was my final chapter. Knightley was coming to stay for the weekend and for a week we had talked for three hours every night on the phone and I had fallen into a wonderful slumber. I really thought that he might be the one, Mr Amazing.

But now, on 13th May 2003 I looked out of my bedroom window at my fabulous view and realised that, yet again. I was going along a learning curve and in fact both of us were. We had shared a wonderful weekend together of closeness. He had been able to see the patterns in the clouds that I saw. We had so many common interests but it wasn't enough. And as he left on the Monday morning I knew that it was really only a one off. And as no response came to my text this confirmed it, as during the past week only a couple of hours would pass between the texts.

He had brought me a whole set of Jane Austen books. And he had read me chapter one of Persuasion. As he read I felt cosy but not enchanted. I just didn't feel what I had with David. I could have gone with it though. He was such a nice man who cared about me. But it wasn't enough for him too. I had enchanted him but he couldn't leave his Surrey roots to come live with me in the Midlands.

I felt disappointed rather than sad. I had so enjoyed his company and I would never have been lonely again, but he felt that I was too much and couldn't contemplate a ready-made family. But this time I still had the friend and I knew that I would always know Knightley. I wouldn't go to the Austen AGM but I would join the Midlands branch instead.

Knightley had been such an interesting person. Working as the odd job man, enjoying the challenge of mending everything and anything but being fascinated by Jane Austen and her writing. He knew so much about her but I felt her.

Since writing this book the happenings have been just incredible and it has always felt that it was someone else that was writing it for me. Knightley and I joked about it being Jane and that she had put a spell on Word so that I couldn't write the last chapter until I had met with Knightley. But as he read her words I didn't feel enchanted. I recognised the strange language that she had used and how frustrated I was that the key character didn't appear in the first chapter.

My friend Pauline had rung to ask if she could have a bed for the night as she had to go to Rochdale and it was too far to get back to London in a day. We sat and talked about the men who had passed through our lives and she asked what was wrong with modern men. I concluded that they liked the idea of intelligent, independent women but when they were faced with the reality they just couldn't handle us.

But Knightley and I had learned a lot about ourselves. We had shared a wonderful closeness but even during that experience I had thought about the man from Oslo and I had wondered about missing my wacky date at the swimming pool when I reached 2,000 hits. And why was it that, every time that I was specifically going out with someone Just Maybe suddenly sent me more emails, some of which were so quirky?'

I concluded that if I had a man who had David's voice, Knightley's closeness and ability to talk about anything and everything, Steve's deep enduring friendship and Just Maybe's mysterious quirkiness that I would have the perfect man.

I had told Just Maybe that this was the last chapter but there were still several weeks until June and a psychic had said that there was a man walking along my path towards me. I thought it was Knightley but she hadn't said that it was someone that I knew. I concluded that my adventure had not finished and I should lie back and just watch the world go by.

Chapter Thirty-seven

On Wednesday, 15th May I had stacks of text from Knightley to the extent that he seemed fractious and so I rang him and we talked for an hour and a half. I had received my mobile phone bill which was embarrassingly high and so decided to contact BT to get on the free calls plan.

So the days went on and we went into deep analysis and realised that it really wasn't doing us any good. We would just have to accept that we really liked each other but that we would have to take each stage at a time.

I had had a nose at the dating sites and had had a couple of emails from the man from Oslo. I had also seen a man who looked quite dishy who turned out to have won the Krypton Factor in 1992 but none of them had the chat of Knightley. So the texts became more frequent once again, and the bedtime calls.

I had been very busy during my three days at work, rushing here there and everywhere, and was finding it interesting but tiring. By saturday I was feeling very weary. I had a period too and I suppose us women have to get on with life but sometimes busy–ness topped with a period just makes life seem a little tough. So on Saturday I was a little topsy turvy and found myself in contact too many times with Knightley .

I had found the Love Calculator on the net; if you want to have fun just look it up and match all and sundry. Goodness knows how it works, 'cos all the matches I did seemed fairly accurate. You match your first name and surname with someone you fancy and see what percentage chance you have of being compatible.

So here's mine.

Knightley 75%

Steve 55%

The Man from Oslo 11%

Just Maybe 74%

But then Knightley, in his cheeky mood, had rather a shock when he matched me with Robbie Williams because we came out as 98% and so Robbie, if you ever read this, you know where your woman is – she's back where your roots are in Staffordshire.

Could it be that Mr Amazing is actually Robbie Williams. I look at his sexy picture on the cover of his book, *Somebody Someday*, and thought, 'Well you do look much older than your years and I am supposed to look quite a bit younger. 'Besides, someone like Robbie probably wouldn't bother about such things.

I had one of those days where it is hard to motivate myself to do anything. So I fiddled on the net and I got flashed by an offer which turned out to be from the Florida tourist board to try to get people back to Florida. It was a good deal and so I decided to go for it but it suddenly brought back sad memories of when I had left Tim. We had organised our dream holiday to Disney and a Caribbean cruise but I had left five weeks before. We did go but it was rather surreal, especially when we went our separate ways when we arrived back at Heathrow.

I rang Knightley and asked him if he wanted to go but he thought I was planning it straight away and said he didn't know whether he would cope with two weeks. I felt low and the past came tumbling back. I texted to say that we shouldn't talk for the rest of the day but of course an hour later was on the phone. He said he would ring me at bedtime but Phoebe and I went to the pictures.

I rang him from the pictures and Phoebe grabbed the phone off me to talk to him. I have always been open with my kids and my men. I have to know that they will get on because I just couldn't live with anyone who they felt uncomfortable with. Of course, everyone has to adapt but there has to be a willingness to compromise. So for Phoebe to want to talk to Knightley was great. My Mr Amazing has to get on with Phoebe and Josh long term. Knightley is very open about whether he would be able to do this or not and so he talked about coming with me, the kids and two of their friends to the caravan in Wales.

So I looked again at the men on the sites.
I had spoken to the psychic on the phone and he had sounded quite nice. I had reached 2000 hits and had a reply from the man to ask when was I going to go to bed with him. I said never.

The whole dating scene seemed to swirl in front of me and I thought of all of those people still looking for Mr or Ms Amazing and my thoughts drifted back to my dear Mr Knightley, who was fuddy duddy in some ways but such a nice person and just seemed so right for me. I thought, 'Did Jane really bring us together?'

Chapter Thirty-eight

'Mum I want to talk to you in private,' Josh said.

Knightley said that he would go away and Josh insisted that I didn't tell Knightley what he had told me. Knightley said that if I did he would go home and Josh knew that I would make Knightley go even if he didn't want to.

I realised that Josh had put me in a dilemma and from that moment I also realised that I could not go on searching any more. I had made some good friends but I had to accept it; if Knightley was not Mr Amazing and ended up purely as a close friend, then that was the way it was going to be.

Josh really was too important. His behaviour at times had been so unbearable recently that I just found it so hard to cope. But I was his mum, a role which I had willingly taken on and, as Knightley talked about not knowing whether he could be part of a couple, I thought, well, I have never really had the closeness that I had always hoped for. Neither David or Tim had really been able to give me that closeness and in fact those few days with Knightley and his openness had meant so much to me.

I thought of how people would be suspicious of a man aged 51 who was still living at home. He had admitted that he had never really had a long-term relationship but he was so open about things, most men just muddled through.

Just Maybe had been divorced for a long time and the man from Oslo had talked about going to a wedding and thinking if only for the party he might like to get married again. But

Knightley thought deeply about things. He had nearly not come to the caravan because he thought that he might not cope. How many men would drive 170 miles to see a woman, stay overnight in the spare room and then drive in the foulest weather to a caravan in North Wales with four children, an additional 110 miles? But Knightley did. He panicked for a few minutes and I said that he didn't have to go but if he didn't he might regret it because he would always want to know if he could have coped. I told him to take his own car and so he did. And two days later I lay on the beach and watched Knightley skim stones with Josh and his friend into the sea and build sandcastles with Phoebe and her friend and I wanted to capture those moments forever.

I really didn't feel that I could ask for more than I had. I just had to accept that my future was already mapped out and I would one day find the end of my story. I was learning something new; how to be patient and enjoy today rather than rushing into tomorrow.

Chapter Thirty-nine

Knightley wouldn't be home for five days as he was finishing off a bathroom at a friend's house and so I said that I would text him as I didn't dare get into the expensive mobile phone bill calls again. I said we could have a long chat when he got home. But I was feeling very naughty and so sent him some suggestive texts which had the right effect. Anyone who prefers talking on a mobile to texting I think is mad. Texting is so much fun and my kids often wondered what I was giggling about or even crying with laughter. Yes, text can certainly brighten up a dull day.

I decided to check my emails and there was only one telling me to look at the men who were looking for me on one of the sites, the one where I had found the man from Oslo or had he found me. I can't really remember but anyhow he had sent me a great long email saying that he hadn't spoken to me for a while and so I went on the site and he was there. We had an amusing discussion as, in the midst of our online conversation, I saw Fluffy and Twotwo our rabbits roaming around the back garden and so told him I was going on a rabbit hunt. Incredibly they decided to go back into the garage where their hutch was and so I was able to continue my discussion with the man from Oslo, which got increasingly funny. He started saying that he was eccentric and so I told him I was too and that, to prove it I had bought a smart car. He said that he loved them.

I then challenged him to the swimming costume date and he said that he would wear his loud American trunks. Well you can imagine the banter and I was in fits of giggles. I thought, wow, not only have I got the nutty Knightley to amuse me but now it looked as though the man from Oslo would amuse me too and with Steve to make the trio, well, I thought what a lucky girl I was.

The rest of the day was taken with amusing text to and from Knightley and so by 10pm I thought... I like this.

Chapter Forty

As the reader knows I have a tendency to go over the top. I suppose I just get excited by the attention that people give me. I had too long being the kid who longed to join the game and now I just want to be me and that's what I told the man from Oslo. If I want to go over the top, well, I want to and if I want to be the quiet thinking woman that I also am, I want to. That's not to say that I can't compromise but when Knightley kept putting blockers in the way I began to think, 'Why do I bother?'

I didn't feel any kind of passion for him and he made it pretty clear that he didn't for me and that he probably never would. If I liked him that much, why did I think about the man from Oslo? So eventually, on 29th May, I told Knightley that he was probably right and that we would be better off as friends. I told the man from Oslo exactly what I was thinking. Besides, Knightly didn't seem to understand why I would feel like crying when it was two days before my daughter Zoe's birthday (she died as a baby 14 years ago).

So after waking up and feeling very hot I decided to do some writing but was going to check my email first. I don't know why I went on the whisper site... well I suppose I did really I was looking for the man from Oslo. He was there at 5.55am and I asked him why he was there; he said that he was always there then and besides it was an hour later in Oslo.

I told him to go to messenger, which Knightley had connected me to, and we had a nice/funny chat. At the end I asked him if he thought we would ever meet and he thought that we would.

The man from Oslo is not the last resort. I would have liked to have met him ages ago, given the chance, but I have decided that there will be no more new men emerging from the sites. Today, 30th May 2003, I have shut down all the dating sites and wait to see who if anyone walks along my path.

Chapter Forty-one

So I deleted all the sites but then I felt bored. I talked to Phoebe about ending my adventure now, as we drove at 10pm to get a Mcflurry for me, Phoebe, Josh and a friend of his who was staying overnight who I had never seen before. I thought it was strange to let your child stay overnight somewhere where you haven't met the mother but I had a chat with the kid's mum and, well, I know that I am not a monster.

So I ate my Mcflurry and went to bed. It was a hot night so I had replaced the duvets with sheets and then of course I woke up cold.

I thought that I would have liked to have been part of the Bloomsbury set with their rampant sex and intellectual discussions but then they might be too much and become a bore. I just had to accept that I was me. I'd only be truly happy if I did.

I got up and logged on, knowing that the man from Oslo would be there and he was. We had a nice hour's chat and he sent me seven photos of himself, some with a beard and some without; I was just about to ask him whether he had one now or not when he disappeared. I suppose he crashed but I decided not to wait around. I liked talking to him; it was completely straight talking with no bullshit. I thought it would be nice to meet him one day but until then I was going to get on with life.

Yesterday I had seen a new short Open University course about Leonardo da Vinci and a couple of others that I was interested in. I thought that my time with the internet dating was nearly up.

I had said to Phoebe that I would finish my adventure with the visit to buy us all a McFlurry saying I was bored. But she said that I shouldn't do that because no one would ever read another of my books if I finished like that. She wanted me to go until the midsummer party and finish there and I suppose she is right. I was going to invite all the men that I had really liked to a mid-summer party and see who came. My suspicion was that none of them would come but it was exciting contemplating it.

In my boredom I had contacted a couple of psychics again and they were really crap. I could have done a much better job of guiding people and thought, like alternative medicine, perhaps I should set up alternative psychic calls at a much more reasonable cost. I could match people for mutual telephone support.

I had had a long email from Pat who I knew through the chat room site. We had talked a couple of times on the phone and she told me about the man that she was seeing about every three weeks. She told me that she was going to be 48 on Saturday and I thought I must remember to send her an ecard.

Yesterday I had one of the most wonderful experiences in my life (that was before I was bored). I had my feet done by a chi-ropodist. Knightley had refused to kiss my feet, so it had spurred me on to do something about my horrible thick toenails. Well, the experience was heavenly, much better than having your hair done and, at £17, a bargain.

Now there's a possible future career – a psychic foot sorter. I wondered what Just Maybe would think of that? He had been quiet again recently. His work seemed to dominate his life too much at the moment and it sounded like a familiar tune.

And as for tunes, the man from Oslo had sent me a pic of when he was a choirboy and had made some suggestive remark about me being into little boys which I adamantly denied. I just told him that he looked sweet, that's all.

Brian at 36 had been too young. He was 53 and was really out of my age range but then he didn't sound at all like an old fogey.

Chapter Forty-two

Yesterday, 31st May, as well as being Zoe's birthday, had been a solar eclipse and the man from Oslo had seen it all in Norway. At the time when I was chatting to him I just envied his experience but later in the day, when Phoebe was doing her homework which coincidentally was about eclipses, I thought, 'What a mean sod not to tell me so I could experience it too, but then he wouldn't have known that I love such things. I absolutely adore and get excited by rainbows and the different stages of the moon. Tim used to know all the different patterns in the stars.

I often have bizarre thoughts like if a tree could think what they would be thinking when it was a windy day and they were being blown around more than usual. Oh yes I think about all sorts of things all of the time.

After I had sent Pat a birthday ecard I sent the man from Oslo a jokey ecard of a kitten which said come and play with me. I thought he would be amused.

He had sent me an email saying that he had abruptly left the site as his eldest son had suddenly appeared nosing over his shoulder while he was having a chat with me. I sent him a reply asking whether he was like Phoebe and Josh, saying, 'Oh Dad, not again'. Of course my suspicious mind said that it was really his wife that appeared so he got off quick but then I thought if that was the case he wouldn't have sent me an explanatory email so quickly.

I thought back to David and all of his deceit but my thoughts were pity for his other woman rather than sadness for me as in many ways he had lived up to his reputation as being a dead loss. Remarkably he had stuck the social work out even through the most traumatic of times but he still hadn't got our website going after promising loads of times and I still had loads of his clutter and some furniture after a period of seven months.

Seven months, that was the time since we had split up and I had done the dating sites for six. And yet it seemed like a lifetime with all the men that I had met online. It was a strange feeling to know that there would not be anyone new.

Knightley had texted me to say that he had a few more hours of work and then he would be going home. He liked telling me what he was doing and I suppose I liked it too.

One of the psychics, in fact a witch, had asked me whether I didn't seek something a little more exciting and I suppose that was the attraction of the man from Oslo and, of course, my mysterious Just Maybe.

The man from Oslo had asked me to send him some photos of me and so after replacing a rabbit-chewed cable with a working, safe one, I got Phoebe to take some pics of me and realised how absolutely disgusting I looked whatever angle she took the pics from. I looked like the before picture. No, I am not gross by any means but, well, my bikini days are well past their sell by date.

I thought of Just Maybe and his gorgeous woman, who I hadn't yet seen a pic of, and justified my flab by saying that I was ten years older then her but all I could say to the man from Oslo was that I wished I was a Muslim and that he could only see my eyes.

Well, I sent some and then thought well what's a bit of flab compared to a great creative mind. The answer was that fewer blokes seemed to consider the great creative mind but then I wanted the one that did.

It was a fabulous sunny day, 28 degrees in London, and I went with the children to buy a pool as well as the computer cable and, just for a joke, I bought a bright red bikini in the sale at ASDA. I then looked even more yuck but then what do I care in my own back garden. I certainly didn't want to attract ten-year-old boys. So, of course , Phoebe said, 'What do you think of Mum's bikini?' to two of Josh's friends and all four of them giggled at me, the cruel bunch. I justify myself by saying I looked great in one once but that was an awful long time ago.

Later that night I sat down and watched a film, *Jerry Maguire*, which has the *Bridget Jones* actress in it. I have seen it before but it's nice sop to watch. Josh cuddled up to me on the settee and it seemed like the old days but then those days can never come again. I have tasted amazing and once tasted its hard not to want to savour again.

I will never be that naïve person again who started on this adventure six months ago. As I watched a text arrived from Knightley to say that he was home. I told him that I was watching a film. The adverts came on and I fuelled up the laptop and saw that there were two emails from Just Maybe. One of them said that he was on Messenger and I would have to invite him to join.

Of course, I didn't understand this if he was already there and asked, via Messenger, Knightley's advice. But that's not really the point; the point is that I have never spoken to Just Maybe and the idea that I will is just so strange.

Chapter Forty-three

It was 9th June and a month since I had physically met Knightley. Neither of us could believe that it was such a short time. We seemed to have known each other for ever and had talked about so many things.

During that month we had been together for equivalent of about a week in two batches and both had not been normal weekends. The first was charging around with Phoebe and Josh doing their plays and the second was the trip to the caravan with four children. Throughout this time Knightley had emphasised our friendship and that he didn't think that he was capable of falling in love. Well, all I could say was that if it wasn't love it was damn nice.

He talked about being a loner and I said that I didn't think that he knew what a loner was. David was a loner and Tim was a loner; in comparison Knightley was nothing like them. They would choose to go to things that interested them on their own. Knightley preferred to go with someone.

So we had had all of these deep discussions and at times it had put me off and I had looked at the man from Oslo with more potential. I looked for him in the mornings and we had brief chats. We had spoken on the phone once and he had said that he would call over the weekend. I had sent him a couple of daft poems but he never made any comment about them and I thought, he is just like the rest unable to tell me what he was really thinking.

Throughout Knightley was always there.

The man from Oslo had said that he would do the swimming pool date and so I set about finding the cozzie. I found an orange and black stripy number with a zip up the front for £2 in a charity shop and started looking for the naff hat to clash nicely with it.

I searched the charity shops wherever I was and then one day I was in Newport and decided to go into the *Newport Advertiser*, the local newspaper to ask their help.

I made my request to the front desk and she told me to go upstairs to the reporters. I went into an open plan room and saw four reporters. I spoke to a youngish woman and started to tell my tale as I gave her my story the other reporters listened in and soon there was a warm giggly exchange between all of us. I had made their day and they agreed to send out a photographer on the Monday to my house to take a picture of me holding the cozzie. They wanted to choose the hat and wished me well with the date. So Monday, 9th June came and after sorting out mounds of ironing which had been lying around, I waited for the man to come and take my pic. I had had to rush up to school in the car because Josh had left his dinner money cheque at home and I didn't want to look at the note saying you have forgotten your dinner money. The photographer arrived .I had been told that he was in his 80s but when I actually saw him I thought what a dishy man for 85 and that if I was 75 I certainly would have been putting on the charms with him, especially as he was available and a widower.

He asked me what the photo was for and said that he might try computer dating. I joked with him about it all but thought if he wanted to he could have his pick of available older widows, my mother included. But then he, like her seemed happy in his memories of his late wife.

Mum had told me that my brother wanted to come and stay on 9th July as that would be a year from the day that Dad had died.

I couldn't believe yet again that it wasn't even yet a year. It seemed such a long time.

My adventure was steaming ahead and was nearly coming to an end and so many things had happened in that time that in many ways it all seemed magical and timeless. It seemed apt that the beginning of the adventure had started with a journalist and now the end was finishing with another. The reporter had taken details of the book and I thought perhaps I would get some free publicity. I thought that I wanted to share this adventure and all of the strong feelings that had gone with it.

I had come out the end happy – not in the dreamy pink glass way that perhaps I had hoped for but in a much deeper way. I knew a lot more about myself and the future looked exciting. I knew that I had to make sure that Josh was happy before I could find my own true happiness but that what I had with Knightley, an increasingly close friendship was what many people dreamed of. One night I sent Knightley a text saying we would never be lonely again and he replied no we wouldn't.

And Steve had sent me a text which implied that he was lonely so I sent a direct reply saying, 'Are you lonely?' He said he was and I replied that I would call him. He was at a conference in Birmingham and was finding it a bore. We exchanged a few texts and then I spoke to him on the phone but he was so tired that he was falling asleep, but he knew I was there and he knew I would always be there for him.

Seeking amazing had brought me these two men, one of which would never be more than a friend, the other who might one day be more but for now we were just there for each other in such an open direct way that Knightley was able to tell me that he thought I should change my hairstyle so that I didn't look like a wild woman. Phoebe described it as mad and thought it suited the mad side of my personality but I agreed with him and succumbed to the fact that, as well as never looking great in a bikini again, my hair would never make me glamorous. But as I started planning the midsummer party I wondered if that was what seeking amazing was about.

Chapter Forty-four

'Night, night girls,' I said as I walked barefoot over the rabbit crap that surrounded Twotwo and Fluffy's hutch. They munched away happily, glancing across at me. It was as if they liked the ritual of me saying night, night to them. I switched off the light, closed the door glancing at the muddle in the garage which still contained so many of David's things and thought how I would enjoy giving it a clear-out once they had all gone.

There was a bright moon as my feet were refreshed by the grass which had grown so quickly in ten days. The man who had cut it after Josh had destroyed the petrol mower by putting petrol in the oil section and the girls had gnawed through the cable of the electric mower, was coming back on Friday and would be shocked by the length. I would just have to pay out again to get them mended or perhaps I could persuade Knightley to mend the electric one.

He was going to see a Chekov play tonight with a friend who had once been a lover and who I thought that he still liked more than a friend. He said that she drove him mad but it was obviously a strange madness to still want to see her.

I had sent an email to the man from Oslo called 'the truth', and had admitted to going over the top and chasing him away just the same as I had done with so many men. I had deleted his email address from my list; as far as I was concerned a man who said that he would ring and then didn't and who didn't send even a text just wasn't worth pursuing. I was disappointed but not mortified. I suppose in my wild dreams I had seen myself spending snowy

Christmas's dressed in warm jolly clothes in Norway with Mum and the kids enjoying it all. It was so nice to dream.

And of course the man from Norway was the one who was going to meet me on the swimming pool date. When the photographer from the local paper had taken my picture I felt like such a fake but I kept my mouth shut. I didn't tell him that it wouldn't happen.

When the journalist rang up to check that the photographer had been and ask for my number so that people could ring me about the swimming hats I didn't say to her that it wasn't going to happen. I just said that, of course, it might not happen. But she said that it would be good if it did and I wished that it would because the idea of it was just so much fun.

I fell asleep on the settee feeling a bit headachey but mainly from talking to Knightley so late the night before. Before I snoozed I had checked my email and there was one from the man from Norway, a long emotional email. He said that I did go over the top and it was off-putting but that I hadn't chased him away. He was sending me an email from an Internet café. His father had had a fall and he had been busy with that and looking for jobs. He sounded distressed and I wanted to send him a virtual hug. I was just so relieved because if nothing else I wanted him as a friend because he understood me and my highs and lows. I knew that I didn't have to go over the top with him any more. I didn't have to attract his attention and whether I met him next week or in a few years time didn't matter because he would respond to me and I to him, showing the most human side to this kind of communication.

I had got to him as he had got to me but whether that would go deeper than being friends only time would tell.

I had put a photo back on the site where I found Just Maybe and Knightley and had a 55 year old send a 'find me attractive' message. I had thought that if I got some emails that it would stop me going over the top with the man from Oslo but I felt nothing and didn't reply to the man.

I thought how a few months ago I would have replied even though he was older than what I was looking for but now I didn't because I thought its easy to just send a pre designed reply but to send an email which poured out your heart and worries for the future like the man from Oslo had taken much more guts.

I had sent the man from Oslo a reply saying that it all felt a little like *A Midsummer Night's Dream* where all the characters are muddled up. As I typed the next part of the adventure one of the words suddenly appeared in italic having not pressed any keys; yet again it felt like someone else was writing the tale which I played a central role in. But this time could it be the Bard himself. Did he and Jane have fun together weaving a story that only they knew the end to? Would there ever be an end? As the moon shone with its three quarters beams the tale became even more and more mysterious.

Chapter Forty-five

I woke to a sunny Friday the 13th and thought, 'Oh, it's my lucky day.' I had never feared Friday the 13ths; they were not bad luck for me.

As I filled a few minutes before Josh woke up, checking to see if Prince Charming had sent me an email, I suddenly heard the announcement sound that the Man from Oslo was available for a chat.

As I've said before men are either not there during this adventure or they arrive in twos and so here I was with two completely different men and fancying both of them. But this time it was fortunate because both wanted me as friends but only Knightley was available for more than distant friendship.

The man from Oslo and I were meant for more but for now he was too busy with elderly relatives and job-seeking and so I didn't have to choose. Potentially I wanted both long term as friends and I knew that whatever happened Knightley and I would always be friends but there was something exciting and intriguing about the man from Oslo. Besides he was the only one who had even considered seriously doing the swimming pool date.

But Knightley was so lovely. For the last few days we had talked for an hour or so in our beds and snuggled down together through the airwaves. Knightley was preparing for his trip up north again to see me and was even braving the idea of taking me and the kids out for a meal. I had warned him of Josh and what a pain in the arse he could be at restaurant meals but then a man who has been on a wet weekend with four kids to a caravan in Wales and still comes back for more must have some reasoning for it and it was nice to know that I was the reason.

I had offered the man from Oslo my spare room if he was job hunting in the North or Midlands. Knightley had wondered whether he should be jealous. The man from Oslo said that he was not a jealous sort. He had an interview for a job he fancied in London and I had joked about being able to do him and Knightley as a job lot. He didn't think that either of them would like that much. I had suggested also that they could share a car to come and see me.

This was the way I was feeling, able to say what I felt and having a good chuckle. Both Knightley and the man from Oslo could be serious and humorous but they both had differing things which made them both attractive and I was enjoying it all. This time I was just going with the flow not going over the top at all and it felt great.

I had such an interesting future to look forward to and I could relax. Close my eyes and just float along on my magic carpet knowing that somehow all the brambles along my route had been cleared and that two men were walking beside me along the path. And so off I went into the sunshine.

I stopped round at Mum's house to pick her up to go to Safeway. She couldn't drive at the moment because she had only recently had a cataract operation. I said that I'd have to buy the local newspaper to see if my story about the swimming hat was in. She said that it was, a male friend of hers had told me. She seemed very wary, but then she has always shied away from all kinds of publicity. Even when I was a child and she and Dad were trying to promote their project of Ikon Gallery in Birmingham they used to be wary of the press. She told me later in the day that she was worried that I would make a fool of myself. I told her that it was just a bit of fun and that most sensible people would see it that way.

So I bought the paper but I didn't see the article for a couple of hours later and I suppose I was surprised because I was on page two; there was a good colour photo of me by the paddling pool and it was well written.

And just as I was curling up for an afternoon snooze to make up for my nocturnal chatting to Knightley, my mobile rang. I swear that this is absolutely true. Like so many things in my adventure an outsider would think that I had made it up.

Well, a woman rang to say that she had my swimming hat. She said that it was orange with great big flowers and plastic things in each flower. But not only did she have the hat; she was very interesting herself. She was 82 years old and she had been on 58 blind dates over a period of two years finishing eight years ago.

She said that she had found her men through the lonely hearts section of the local newspaper. If you could have seen my grin you would have thought that my face would split. I found that for several hours I just went around chuckling. I said I would ring her in the morning and visit her with Phoebe as I thought Phoebe would enjoy coming with me. Life was getting so much fun.

So I rang the newspaper to tell them that I had a follow-up story but the reporter who had written it was on leave for the day. The receptionist, however, knew who I was straight away and said that the reporter would be in touch on Monday.

I got two copies of the paper and I sent one to Knightley to show his friends who had met through the Internet and I posted the other one off to Norway to surprise the man from Oslo. OK the cozzie wouldn't be a surprise but I wouldn't show him the hat.

Chapter Forty-six

I always have great intentions of getting things done but of course there are usually more interesting things to distract me and so on the day of the midsummer party I was still sorting the house when I should have been getting food ready.

My friend from down south arrived at 4pm, as she said she would, and immediately mucked in with the cooking. Knightley had been here since Thursday night and was a trooper just helping out with everything and anything.

The meal had gone fine; there was a playground just outside and so while Knightley and I had a starter, which Phoebe and Josh declined, they went to play.

There are some things in life that you dearly miss as a lone parent and Knightley did something which was so nice, and to readers may seem so simple; he went to get the children from the playground while I sat waiting for the main course. Knightley is that kind of man, in fact he is kind. He is cautious, not knowing how he feels, and won't just let go but then I think of all the unhappy men who have fallen in love with the wrong women and have spent their lives in misery. Just Maybe had fallen in love with a woman who shunned his love,

Whatever Knightley thinks he feels for me, he shows warmth towards me and he is also incredibly funny. Since meeting up with him I think I have laughed more than I have for years.

Anyhow, it was Midsummers day and I was coming to the end of my adventure. Anything that happened after midnight would be the next episode in my life. Steve was one of the first people to arrive and as I predicted Knightley and Steve got on well together. I have always regarded Steve as just a close friend and in fact more like a brother but he admitted during the evening that I could have been more to him. He flirted most of the evening with my southern friend but he also knew that she was well attached.

Poor Steve he is such a lovely man but just doesn't seem to be able to find the right woman. Although he admitted to wondering what might have been with me, he also has this burning desire to be a dad again and is seeking a woman who is young and willing to have children.

The party progressed and local people mixed with my old friends and my two Internet men. They both chuckled when I introduced them as such.

One local friend had to go home early but she later rang desperately wanting to know which of the two men was the favoured one. When I said it was Knightley she was pleased and said that he seemed a nice person and he is.

But I still wandered about the man from Oslo. Was Knightley the right man for me, with his over-cautious nature that put me off to a certain extent, or should I just wait for the man from Oslo. I certainly didn't want to start searching for someone new.

I had had my six months and it had been an interesting time but it was long enough.

We had games in the garden. Table tennis on the patio, a badminton net tied between the trees, croquet at the bottom of the garden and an array of hoops and ra ra things lying near the conservatory door. As people arrived they were given a piece of chalk to draw a picture or write a message on the slabs.

The weather had been beautiful but just before the party there had been a sprinkling of rain. It didn't spoil the party though and I felt so happy as I mixed amongst the people I liked to know and watched children and adults mingling together, both new and old friends. I had come a long way from the misery caused by my isolation with David and I just felt so alive.

As midnight came I knew that although my journey would continue that it would now be my own private personal journey, one that might be shared but not in this intense way that the last six months has been shared with you.

I thought back to Clive who had spurred me to seek amazing and wandered how he was. I had sent him an email to tell him what I was doing but he hadn't replied.

I thought of all of the men that I had met along this journey and all of their personal stories and ideals. And I knew that for some it would be a journey of disappointment and heartache with no one there to hold their hands or comfort them when things went wrong. But for others they may actually find what they had always hoped for.

A Happy Ending

Christmas had been lovely, one of the nicest I had ever had. The magic was no longer there but the closeness and warmth was the nicest present that I could ever have.

On 30th December 2003, a magical date, we stopped to set off seven helium balloons with our messages out to sea from Southport.

It was a cold night and Mum sat in the car until the very last moment.

The three children excitedly wrote their messages and we helped tie them on.

We had had a great day and Mum had even paddled in the freezing cold sea, now it was coming to an end and we would soon be on our way home.

As the balloons floated off together I snuggled closely up to Knightley and knew that I had found my Mr Amazing and I was so very lucky.

I later thought of my journey and was so glad that it had come to an end. I thought of Steve and Just Maybe and just hoped that they could be as happy as me and my Mr Knightley.

And Finally I heard from Clive, the Hack again and am keeping in touch. He is happy for me but still searching so if you fancy tall, slim, good looking with a flair for writing then email me and I'll let him know. Or if you are one of the men I met on my journey I would love to hear from you to find out what happened next.

rachelbramble@yahoo.co.uk

ALSO AVAILABLE BY RACHEL BRAMBLE

THE NAMELESS SOCIAL WORKER

CLASSIFICATION: Autobiography/Social Interest
FORMAT: Paperback
PAGE EXTENT: 243pp
PUBLICATION DATE: September 2004
SIZE: A5

£8.99

ISBN 1 85756 519 3

The Nameless Social Worker represents not only the author herself, but all those dedicated individuals within social work whose invaluable service to the community all too often goes unrecognised. The author, a social worker for over twenty years, examines the attitude of society, and in particular the media, towards social work and suggests why the profession and the services it provides are often under-appreciated or misconstrued. The author also argues, however, that the profession itself – including the bureaucratic machinery underpinning (and often hampering) its service delivery to clients – is equally responsible for its public portrayal. In this she gives us the benefit of her vast personal experience and puts forward her philosophy for the profession as a whole becoming more self-assured and less introverted, working with the media and the community in improving its public perception, rather than shying away from them like the proverbial mouse before the roaring lion. The book is also valuable as a fascinating and emotional insight into one woman's life, family and career.

The Author
Rachel Bramble entered the field of social work thirty years ago through a number of different circumstances and has worked with all sorts of different people, many of whom have needed support. She has had her own share of ups and downs, most importantly coping with the loss of her first much wanted child through a sudden infant death. She quotes herself as being an ordinary person with some extraordinary tales to tell.

Janus Publishing Company, 105-107 Gloucester Place, London W1U 6BY. http://www.januspublishing.co.uk

JANUS